Wings Over The Alaska Highway

Wings Over
The Alaska Highway

Bruce McAllister

Peter Corley-Smith

Roundup Press

BOULDER, COLORADO, U.S.A.

Roundup Press
P.O. Box 109
Boulder, CO 80306-0109
USA

Library of Congress Control Number: 2001087894
ISBN 0-9638817-7-9

Cover and book design: Jim Brennan
Photography editor: Bruce McAllister

Distributed in the U.S. by
Roundup Press
(303) 444-9484
mcax@aol.com
http://www.wingsalcan.com

Distributed in Canada by
Sono Nis Press
PO Box 5550, Stn. B
Victoria, BC V8R 6S4
tel: (250) 598-7807
sono.nis@islandnet.com
http://www.islandnet.com/sononis/

Printed and bound in Canada by Friesens

Disclaimer

The authors have attempted to be accurate in listing aeronautical information (including runway lengths, coordinates, airport/airstrip conditions and warnings). We cannot be held responsible for the accuracy of this information and it is not be used for navigational purposes. Current government charts, approach plates, booklets, and local pilots should be consulted for accurate information.

All Color Photography by Bruce McAllister
unless otherwise noted.

Acknowledgements

Jamie Anderson, Paul Bachinger, Jack Baker, Murray Biggin, Stan Bridcut, Earl Brown, Bob Cameron, Gordon Cameron, Doug Champlin, Charles Estlin, Reg Forbes, Sam Harrel, Walter Houghton, Celia Hunter, Gary Kimpinski, Paula and Don Lounsbury, Sheldon Luck, Don Lumsden, Martin Lynch, Mac and Maggie McMahon, Doris and Herman Peterson, John and Josie Piety, Amy Prosser, Jim Ruotsala, Sylvie Savage, Clark Seaborn, Howard Smiley, Sam Side, Bob Trail and Bob Turner.

Photo Credits:

FRONT COVER: A-26 Fire Bomber with full load of slurry, headed for a hot spot in the Yukon. August, 1974.

BACK COVER: In a Piper Super Cub, a US Fish & Wildlife biologist/pilot is doing a dall sheep census in Alaska in 1968. Canadian and US biologists often cross borders on joint research projects—from the Plains to the Arctic.

PAGE 2: Liard River Airport.

The aerial photographs on the following pages © Her Majesty the Queen in Right of Canada, reproduced with permission of the National Air Photo Library with permission of Natural Resources Canada.
Page 12 © 1984, A-26584-15
Page 93 © 1985, A-26606-120
Page 196 © 1995, A-31727-75
Page 199 © 1985, A-26835-30
Page 200 © 1952, A13476-102
Page 202 © 1975, A-24208-45

In Memory of
Howard Smiley and J. B. Reeves

ALONG THE ALCAN

Plunging through the wilderness like a determined prospector, the Alaska-Canada Military Highway (Alcan) was built at eight miles a day during World War II to counter any invasion by Japanese forces—who thanked workers in a propaganda broadcast for opening a way for their own troops. Rather than forging a more direct route to Alaska, planners linked existing airfields at Fort St. John, Fort Nelson, Watson Lake, and Whitehorse.

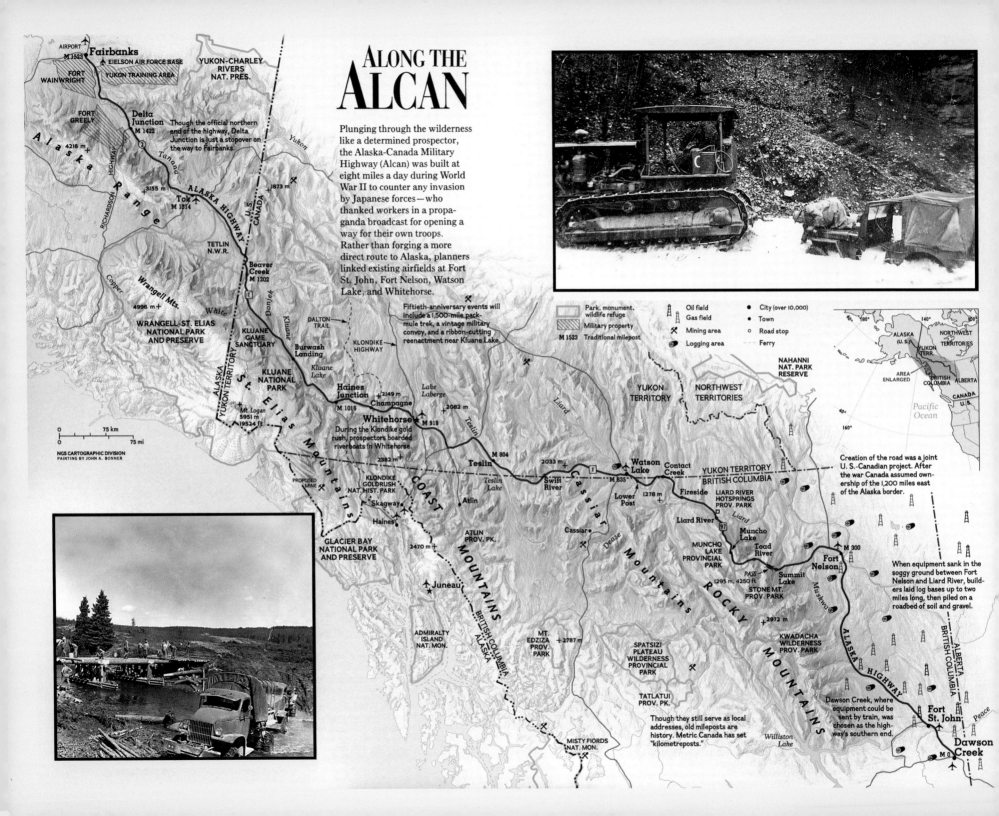

Fiftieth-anniversary events will include a 1,500-mile pack-mule trek, a vintage military convoy, and a ribbon-cutting reenactment near Kluane Lake.

Though the official northern end of the highway, Delta Junction is just a stopover on the way to Fairbanks.

During the Klondike gold rush, prospectors boarded riverboats in Whitehorse.

Creation of the road was a joint U.S.-Canadian project. After the war Canada assumed ownership of the 1,200 miles east of the Alaska border.

When equipment sank in the soggy ground between Fort Nelson and Liard River, builders laid log bases up to two miles long, then piled on a roadbed of soil and gravel.

Though they still serve as local addresses, old mileposts are history. Metric Canada has set "kilometreposts."

Dawson Creek, where equipment could be sent by train, was chosen as the highway's southern end.

Legend

- ☐ Park, monument, wildlife refuge
- ▨ Military property
- M 1523 Traditional milepost
- ⚒ Oil field
- ⚒ Gas field
- ✕ Mining area
- ⛏ Logging area
- ● City (over 10,000)
- ▪ Town
- ○ Road stop
- --- Ferry

Place names and features

Fairbanks — M 1523
AIRPORT
EIELSON AIR FORCE BASE
FORT WAINWRIGHT
YUKON TRAINING AREA
YUKON-CHARLEY RIVERS NAT. PRES.
FORT GREELY
Delta Junction — M 1422
4216 m
Alaska Range
RICHARDSON HIGHWAY
3155 m
Tanana
Tok — M 1314
1873 m
ALASKA HIGHWAY
TETLIN N.W.R.
U.S. CANADA
Yukon
Beaver Creek — M 1202
Copper
White
Wrangell Mts.
4996 m
WRANGELL-ST. ELIAS NATIONAL PARK AND PRESERVE
KLUANE GAME SANCTUARY
ALASKA / YUKON TERRITORY
St. Elias Mountains
Donjek
DALTON TRAIL
KLONDIKE HIGHWAY
Kluane
Burwash Landing
Kluane Lake
KLUANE NATIONAL PARK
Haines Junction — M 1016
2149 m
Champagne
Mt. Logan 5951 m 19524 ft
Lake Laberge
2082 m
Whitehorse — M 918
2382 m
KLONDIKE GOLDRUSH NAT. HIST. PARK
Skagway
Haines
COAST MOUNTAINS
Teslin
Teslin Lake
Atlin
M 804
2033 m
Swift River
ATLIN PROV. PK.
Cassiar
Dease
Cassiar Mountains
Watson Lake
M 835
Contact Creek
Lower Post
1278 m
Fireside
Liard River
Liard
YUKON TERRITORY / BRITISH COLUMBIA
LIARD RIVER HOTSPRINGS PROV. PARK
Muncho Lake
Toad River
MUNCHO LAKE PROVINCIAL PARK
PASS 1295 m, 4250 ft
Summit Lake
STONE MT. PROV. PARK
2972 m
KWADACHA WILDERNESS PROV. PARK
Fort Nelson — M 300
Muskwa
ROCKY MOUNTAINS
ALASKA HIGHWAY
97
ALBERTA / BRITISH COLUMBIA
Fort St. John
Peace
Dawson Creek — M 0

GLACIER BAY NATIONAL PARK AND PRESERVE
Juneau
BRITISH COLUMBIA / ALASKA
ADMIRALTY ISLAND NAT. MON.
2470 m
MT. EDZIZA PROV. PARK
2787 m
SPATSIZI PLATEAU WILDERNESS PROVINCIAL PARK
TATLATUI PROV. PK.
MISTY FIORDS NAT. MON.
Williston Lake

YUKON TERRITORY
NORTHWEST TERRITORIES
NAHANNI NAT. PARK RESERVE

Inset locator map

AREA ENLARGED
ALASKA (U.S.)
YUKON TERR.
NORTHWEST TERRITORIES
BRITISH COLUMBIA
ALBERTA
CANADA / U.S.
Pacific Ocean
180° 160° 140° 120° 100°
40° 60°

NGS CARTOGRAPHIC DIVISION
PAINTING BY JOHN A. BONNER

75 km
75 mi

CONTENTS

Map of the Alaska Highway.
—© NATIONAL GEOGRAPHIC SOCIETY

CAT rescuing Jeep in fast flowing river near Ft. Nelson, 1942.
—GLENBOW ARCHIVES, CALGARY, AB, NA-1796-26

Building a bridge near Ft. Nelson, 1942.
—YUKON ARCHIVES/MACBRIDE MUSEUM VOL. 1, 3553

Introduction

Ås early as 1940, the United States and Canadian governments were becoming increasingly concerned about the growing aggressiveness of Japan. That year, President Franklin D. Roosevelt and Prime Minister Mackenzie King agreed to establish a Permanent Joint Board on Defence to co-ordinate military planning and prepare for any potential attacks along the north Pacific coast. Canada began at once with the construction of airports along a route to Alaska, to be known as the Northwest Staging Route. The Japanese attack on Pearl Harbor in December 1941 prompted the US not only to follow suit but initiate construction of a military road to Alaska. Debate about the best route to follow was cut short when the military decided that it should follow the Northwest Staging Route to utilize air support.

This famous World War II poster typified the indomitable will and determination that the U.S. and Canada brought to every phase of the war effort—from the Home Front, to spectacular projects like the building of the Alaska Highway.

—NATIONAL ARCHIVES

The construction of the Alaska Highway was a classic example of American ability to organize and complete an exceptionally difficult engineering project in short order. The first problem was to select a route. The residents of British Columbia, the Yukon and Alaska all wanted a coastal route to tie in with sea transport. The military wanted it to be far enough inland to be safe from potential Japanese air attacks. Canada as a whole favoured a route along the Rocky Mountain Trench, mainly because this would provide the fewest engineering and construction problems. As we shall see, the eventual choice would depend on the availability of functional airports, some of which had already been constructed by the Canadian government before the Japanese attacked Pearl Harbor.

By almost any yardstick, the creation of the Alaska Highway was a remarkable organizational and engineering achievement. Little was known about the country to be traversed except that it was generally and accurately described as rugged wilderness and that it would certainly be challenging. Where it wasn't heavily forested, mountains, muskeg, lakes, rivers and swamps would have to be circumvented or overcome. Starting virtually from scratch, the American military—more particularly the US Army Corps of Engineers—assembled the thousands of troops (some 10,000 in all, many of them African-Americans from the southern States) required for the task. These troops all had to be transported by one of three routes: train to the northwestern railhead in Dawson Creek, a remote farming community in the Peace River district of British Columbia; by sea to Skagway, then by the White Pass & Yukon Route railway to Whitehorse; or by sea through Valdez and on to Fairbanks and Big Delta. As well, private-sector contractors moved in thousands of construction workers.

The number of planes being ferried (the majority destined for Russia) jumped by over 1000%, from 311 to 3,273, between 1942 and 1944.

Alaska and the final decision that this should be done. From April 1942 on, proposal followed proposal and one negotiation succeeded another. The Soviet representatives were as difficult as usual to deal with, refusing today an offer which they had seemed to accept yesterday, only to revive it on the morrow.

The Russians' objections were understandable but not sustainable. Understandable because the Alaska-Siberia (ALSIB) route meant Russia would have to establish and supply many airfields "if the planes delivered via Alaska were ultimately to reach the fighting front."

John Czekala (L) and Byron McMahon served with the 7th Ferry Group during World War II. McMahon flew one of the A-20s on their first ferry flight up the Alaska Highway. On the first attempt, bad weather claimed one of the A-20s near Lethbridge, Alberta.
–Courtesy Steve Shirley

Unsustainable because "the alternates—the waterborne route to Archangel, along which German bombers and submarines took heavy toll, and the air-water route by way of the Persian Gulf, where greater distance and the abrasive qualities of wind-blown African soil lessened the life of planes and engines.

"But the United States was persistent, the Soviet need for aircraft was real, the advantages of the northern air route were apparent, and on 3 August 1942 the Soviet government agreed that it could be used. Within three weeks the AAF was to deliver fifty A-20s [Havoc], twelve B-25s [Mitchell], forty-three P-40s [Warhawk] and fifty P-39s [Airacobra] into Soviet hands at Fairbanks.

"Yet another backtracking by the Russians again delayed the deliveries, but, by September 3, the first five lend-lease A-20s reached Fairbanks. "Soviet personnel had assembled at Ladd Field; Russian pilots received instruction on the American aircraft; and on 29 September the first planes accepted by the Soviet Military Mission in Alaska took off for Nome and Siberian points."[3]

The Russians, evidently, were not sentimental. When one Russian pilot was reported missing between Fairbanks and Nome, the American air search and rescue unit of the Alaska Air Transport Command offered assistance to the Russians. The Russian senior officer in Alaska is quoted as responding with the equivalent of "thanks but no thanks—he wasn't a very good pilot, anyway."[4]

Nor, apparently, were Russian pilots unduly diffident: "One cocky Russian landed a P-39 fighter at one of the waystops and at high speed taxied it among parked planes. The American

Arriving at the ATC's Alaskan Division base at Nome, Alaska on Easter Sunday, 1944, Brig. Gen. Dale V. Gaffney, Commanding General of the Alaskan Division (L), gets a handshake from Col. N. S. Vasin, commander of the Russian detachment there.
–K. Kennedy Collection, 91-098-845, Archives, University of Alaska, Fairbanks

The first Russian military mission to Alaska arrived at Nome in late Summer of 1942. Note that officers from both sides came in a variety of breeches.
–K. Kennedy Collection, 91-098-851N, Archives, University of Alaska, Fairbanks

Civilian employee Helen Roberts painting a red star on a lend-lease air transport. The layout for the star was copied from a Texaco gas station logo.

–K. KENNEDY COLLECTION, 91-098-861N, ARCHIVES, UNIVERSITY OF ALASKA, FAIRBANKS

Final check on a Douglas A-20 Havoc attack bomber before take-off for Siberia. All three men are Russians, but the one on left is wearing a Gaffney jacket, named after General Gaffney, the top general in the Alaskan Division, ATC.

–K. KENNEDY COLLECTION, 91-098-850N, ARCHIVES, UNIVERSITY OF ALASKA, FAIRBANKS

operations officer caught up with him and gave him hell. The pilot, unimpressed, said, 'I got eight Nazi planes. How many you got?'"[5]

Evidently, though, according to another writer, Richard Ecke, quoting from an interview with ferry pilot Byron McMahon, the Russians could be very congenial: "In Alaska, Russians greeted American pilots with a ready supply of vodka. Whenever we'd take a flight up there there'd be a big party hosted by the Russians…on the other hand, they were very stern in daylight."[6]

Russian women fighter pilots in Siberia, some of whom may have flown lend-lease aircraft. One of their own, Lily Litvyak, shot down seven German aircraft before she met her end in combat.

–Tass from Sovphoto

A crash just short of Nome, but the aircraft was repaired and eventually reached the Russian-German front. Aircraft such as this P-39Q often had hydraulic problems.

–K. Kennedy Collection, 91-098-870, Archives, University of Alaska, Fairbanks

Flights to reinforce US air defences in Alaska started in January. By the end of 1942 close to 300 military aircraft had reached Alaska, but of those, less than 150 were turned over to the Soviet Union. Other aircraft, both military and civilian, never made it to Alaska—mostly because of bad weather. Thereafter, "the number of planes being ferried (the majority destined for Russia) jumped by over 1000%, from 311 to 3,273, between 1942 and 1944. The total amount of traffic ran almost twice as high."[7]

The Russians honored the P-39's role in World War II by rebuilding this one in the Russian Air Force museum at Monino, near Moscow.
—Courtesy Doug Champlin, Champlin Fighter Museum, Mesa, AZ

The "Million-Dollar Valley" gained this name in the first rush, when unfamiliar mountain terrain and tough weather broke up entire squadrons of bombers and fighters headed up the Northwest Staging Route to Fairbanks—some later to be handed over to the Russians. Two squadrons of Martin B-26 Marauders headed north in bad weather on January 16, 1942. One flight of three bombers lost its way. The pilots very sensibly decided to make an emergency landing on the snow in a wide valley before they ran out of fuel. Spotted two days later by the leader of a flight of P-40 fighters heading west, the crews were rescued by Russ Baker, a Canadian bush pilot, with a ski-equipped aircraft. Only the engines and some ancillary equipment could be salvaged at the time, hence the ironic "Million-Dollar Valley" nickname.

P-39

Bell *Airacobra*

U. S. Army Interceptor Pursuit

COMPLIMENTS · VISUAL
TRAINING DEPARTMENT
· · BELL AIRCRAFT CORP. · ·
U. S. A.

Nevertheless, after a rocky start, assistance to the Russians was substantial. Historian Blake Smith records that deliveries of aircraft over this route from 1942 to 1945 consisted of 5,066 fighters, 1,495 bombers, 711 transports and 54 training aircraft.[8] It was a substantial contribution to the Allied war effort against Germany.

P-39 Training Dept. profile from Bell Aircraft.
—Courtesy Denver Public Library, Western History Collection

A Beech F-2 (modified Beech 18) equipped for aerial mapping photography was used to determine some of the Alaska Highway routing.

—Courtesy Don F. Tomlinson, USAAF Photo

Aviation's Role In Building the Alaska Highway

Civil Aviation had a commanding influence on the decision over the final route of the Alaska Highway. In 1935, during the worst of the Great Depression years, the celebrated Canadian bush pilot, Punch Dickins, flew two senior government bureaucrats on an impressively long aerial survey flight. His passengers were Deputy Minister of Mines Dr. Charles Camsell and Daniel McLean, the Defence Department's civil inspector of western airways. They were looking for mining information and potential sites for airfields to provide air corridors in the

From the beginning of the project, aviation played a most important role.

A Fokker Universal moored in the Fraser River, Prince George, British Columbia in the fall of 1933. Grant McConachie is shoveling and Stan (Limey) Green is the watchful engineer.
—GLENBOW ARCHIVES, CALGARY, AB, NA-2097-64

The crew of a Cordova Air Services Bellanca about to embark on a photo mapping mission.
—L. WASHBURN COLLECTION, 82-58-112, ARCHIVES, UNIVERSITY OF ALASKA, FAIRBANKS

northwest. Starting from Edmonton, they flew down the Mackenzie River as far as Aklavik, in its delta, across the Yukon into Alaska, then back down through the Yukon and British Columbia, over to Fort Simpson, on the Mackenzie River again, north to Coppermine, on the shore of Coronation Gulf, and back to Edmonton—a total of approximately 8,700 miles (14 000 km).[9]

Meanwhile, private enterprise was working towards the same goal. G. W. G. (Grant) McConachie of Yukon Southern Air Transport had his sights set on a modified great circle route to the Orient: Edmonton, Prince George, Fort St. John, Fort Nelson, Watson Lake and on to Whitehorse. Eventually, he hoped to take this route through Alaska, across Bering Strait and then south to China.

During one of his cross-country flights in 1938 he landed at the Northern Trading Company's

Another muddy stretch (going two feet deep) far north of Fort. St. John.
—AP/WIDE WORLD PHOTOS

Blasting at Muncho Lake.
—Glenbow Archives, Calgary, NA-1796-32

post at Fort Liard, just east of the Yukon-Northwest Territories border. There he met Jack Baker, who had trapped for many years in the Mackenzie Delta and come south to become a trader. An enterprising individual, Baker, using a self-help manual, had fabricated his own radio so that he could communicate with the Hudson's Bay Company's post manager at Fort Nelson. Much impressed, McConachie offered him a job to open up a radio station at Watson Lake—a requirement for McConachie to win a government airmail contract through to Whitehorse.

Baker was dropped off at the lake by bush pilot Ralph Oakes in February 1939 and made

good progress, although he and George Watson, the only resident—a Yorkshireman after whom

the lake is named—and a man named Thompson, worked by themselves. Then, in 1940, the

Canadian government moved a crew in to build a runway and equip Watson Lake with lights

and radio communications. Jack Baker moved on to become Yukon Southern's chief dispatcher

in Whitehorse. McConachie had put a similarly slender crew into Fort Nelson, and they, too,

had made progress with a crude but usable landing strip when a government crew took over.

The arrival of the construction crews in 1940 marked the beginning of what came to be

known as the Northwest Staging Route. The United States had become increasingly concerned

Colonel J.A. O'Connor, US Army engineer in charge of the southern sector of the Alaska Highway construction, in radio communication with a fellow officer far ahead in the wilderness.
–AP/WIDE WORLD PHOTOS

Tough mud between Pickhandle Lake and Beaver Creek, Yukon. This section was not finished until 1943. Convoys previously had to be towed through.
NATIONAL ARCHIVES

about the growing military strength and aggressiveness of Japan; and both the US and Canada realized that they had no air bases in the northwest from which to mount any defence, either along the coast or inland into Alaska and the Yukon. The first step was to establish the Canada-United States Permanent Joint Board on Defence—and the board's first decision was to set up a string of air bases stretching from Edmonton, Alberta, to Fairbanks, Alaska: Grand Prairie (250 miles [400 km]), Dawson Creek (62 miles [100 km]), Fort St. John (46 miles [74 km]), Fort Nelson (272 miles [440 km]), Watson Lake (345 miles [550 km]), Whitehorse (273 miles [440 km]), Northway (346 miles [560 km]), and Fairbanks (262 miles [420 km]). (Later, a number of emergency airstrips were added along the route). The next stage, of course, after

An army truck and grader on the Teslin River Ferry Crossing near Johnson's Crossing.
—Yukon Archives, H. Pepper Collection, 17

A 4-ton truck being winched out of the Takhini River. It was loaded with beer for the 4th of July celebrations at a military construction camp in 1942.
—Yukon Archives, R. Hays Collection, 5689

Grading in progress during construction of the Alaska Highway near Goose Bay, Kluane Lake (west of Haines Junction), August 1943.
—National Archives

An old food cache, in 1968, near Burwash landing on Kluane Lake.

the jolt of the Japanese attack on Pearl Harbor in December 1941, was to use these bases to facilitate the construction of the Alaska Highway, which began in 1942.

From the beginning of the project, aviation played a most important role. One man, in particular can be singled out. His name was Les Cook, a bush pilot flying a Noorduyn Norseman for the British Yukon Navigation Company's White Pass Airways out of Whitehorse. Colonel William Hoge, of the US Army Corps of Engineers, recruited Cook to do what was very much a pathfinding reconnaissance to establish a route. Historian Ken Coates records that

> Les Cook proved to be an inspired choice. After a series of flights, Hoge gradually learned the lay of the land and was able to sketch out a preliminary route. Hoge later said, "Les Cook was the great one. Les took me every place. He went between the mountains.... I got to know the country pretty well." With Cook's help, Hoge determined that the best route crossed the mountains about 80 miles [130 km] east of Teslin, in the southern Yukon. One of the major routing problems had been set to rest.[10]

However, the usefulness of aviation in building the highway was a two-way street; it was also a boon to the bush-flying companies in the area. In Canada during the 1930s, the Post Office Department had consistently refused to grant adequate airmail contracts to flying companies, a benefit granted to nearly all such companies throughout the western world to help them establish routes and airports with radio and lighting facilities. Consequently, an era of fierce competition had prevailed, curtailing the growth of aviation.

Then, in 1938, the government enacted legislation to create Trans-Canada Air Lines, Canada's first transcontinental airline, and awarded the new crown corporation very generous airmail contracts. Benefits to other companies soon followed. That same year, Yukon Southern Air Transport won a contract to fly mail from Vancouver and Edmonton to Whitehorse. By 1942, when construction of the Alaska Highway began, the Canadian Pacific Railway, in the interests of serving a national wartime emergency and with government approval, amalgamated 10 bush-flying companies, firstly to ameliorate the cut-throat competition and secondly to stabilize the aviation industry in Canada.

A US military floatplane on Kluane Lake during the Highway construction in 1942.
—YUKON ARCHIVES, MACBRIDE COLLECTION, VOL. 2/3881

A US Navy Alaskan Survey crew that mapped large areas of Alaska in the 1930s without a fatal mishap.
—S. R. CAPPS COLLECTION, 83-149-2911N, ARCHIVES, UNIVERSITY OF ALASKA, FAIRBANKS

Wartime military truck (left) showing its age. On display at the Norman Wells Museum, it is one of the last visible signs of World War II in this area.

First military truck to make it from Whitehorse to Fairbanks during construction of the Alaska Highway cut it close to the end of 1942.
–Yukon Archives, R.A. Carter Collection, 1501

The new company became Canadian Pacific Air Lines. But before this amalgamation was consummated, four aviation companies were operating in BC and the Yukon: the British Yukon Navigation Company's White Pass Airways in Whitehorse, and Northern Airways in Carcross. In BC, there were Canadian Airways in Fort St. James and Yukon Southern Air Transport which, by then, was operating a scheduled airline from Edmonton and Vancouver through to Whitehorse in addition to its bush flying out of Prince George and Fort St. James. The airline provided relatively consistent access for personnel into the area and the bush-flying companies were in constant demand to move people and supplies to isolated construction camps, as well as to evacuate sick or injured personnel.

On the Alaska side of the border, similar conditions prevailed: numerous small aviation companies with little or no federal support were busy fighting each other for survival. In

1937, Governor John W. Troy reported that "Alaskan aviation is out of the pioneering stage." It was now composed of 40 companies and 101 pilots.[11] The competition between these companies had become so intense that "It became a tough, cutthroat game and appeared that no one was going to make a living. The operators formed an organization, a sort of gentleman's agreement setting fares, freight rates and charter rates. Suddenly one operator seemed to be getting all the business. He had been the organizer of the agreement, and now he was cutting all his prices."[12]

Relief for the Alaska aviation companies came in the same year as for Canada. It came in the form of the Civil Aeronautics Act of 1938. Before then, "most legislation specifically *excluded* Alaska, leaving the northern territory without assistance that aided the economic build-up of other states."[13] Now federal funds would be available to build airports with navigation aids, as well as providing operating subsidies and airmail contracts. By 1942, construction of the Alaska Highway, and its associated Northwest Staging Route airports, dramatically improved the funds available for these improvements.

Many companies were involved. The principal ones were Pan American Airways, Northern Consolidated Airlines, Wien Consolidated Airlines, Northwest Airlines and Delta Airlines, much of the flying being done by the elite of Alaska bush pilots—some of whom will be highlighted later. To add to this bonanza, the Canol Pipeline provided, at the end of the long Depression years, much appreciated revenue flying.

The Canol project was initiated at the same time as the Alaska Highway was being constructed, mainly to provide fuel for all the heavy equipment required for that construction,

Aviation led the way in providing transport, as well as providing invaluable knowledge of these areas and such obvious assistance as preliminary reconnaissance for the routes those roads ultimately took.

At Nenana on the Tanana River: barrels of fuel waiting for trans-shipment to the Interior. Before the Canol Pipeline was completed, much fuel had to come in by river.
—Kansas State Historical Society, Topeka, KS

Norman Wells (facing page) on the MacKenzie River, was the source of oil for the Canol Pipeline. In recent times some islands (above right) were man-made and used as drilling pads.

and to provide fuel to the airfields along the Northwest Staging Route. It involved an expansion of the existing oil fields at Norman Wells on the Mackenzie River, and the construction of a 600-mile-long (965-km) pipeline to a new refinery at Whitehorse. From Whitehorse, a smaller pipeline would be built alongside the new highway to Ladd Field, the Army Air Force base at Fairbanks. Supplying both projects—the Alaska Highway and the Canol Pipeline—became a profitable source of revenue for Northern Airways, as well as several other operators in the far northwest.

The civilian companies that won the contract for Canol, a consortium called Bechtel-Price-Callahan, was refreshingly candid in its advertisement for construction labourers:

June 15 42

THIS IS NO PICNIC

Working and living conditions on this job are as difficult as those encountered on any construction job ever done in the United States or foreign territory. Men hired for this job will be required to work and live under the most extreme conditions imaginable. Temperatures will range from 90 degrees above zero to 70 degrees below zero. Men will have to fight swamps, rivers, ice and cold. Mosquitoes, flies and gnats will not only be annoying but will cause bodily harm. If you are not prepared to work under these and similar conditions

DO NOT APPLY

Welding crew at Mile 273 from Johnson's Crossing, early 1944.
—Yukon Archives, R. Finnie Collection, 81/21-465

Started in 1942, the pipeline, with an accompanying road, was completed in February 1944, another triumph over climate and topography. However, for a number of reasons, it was

The MacKenzie River, south of Norman Wells.

Alaska Highway Milepost, taken in 1968.

far from a success and the refinery at Whitehorse was shut down in April 1945. Because of the remoteness of the construction camps, much of the heavy equipment was left to rust in the bush.

Here, again, aircraft had been invaluable both before and during construction and, as was invariably the case in the hitherto isolated sub-Arctic northwest wilderness, aviation led the way in providing transport, as well as providing invaluable knowledge of these areas and such obvious assistance as preliminary reconnaissance for the routes those roads ultimately took.

CHAPTER 3

The Trench

The north end of the Trench (top right)
lines up with Scoop Lake (upper center)
and headwaters of the mighty Liard River.

As mentioned earlier, the Rocky Mountain Trench between Prince George and Watson Lake was the first choice of the Canada-United States Permanent Joint Board on Defence. It was easily the preferred route because it is a straight, deep valley stretching 430 miles (690 km) between the two. Consequently, from the practical, engineering point of view, the Trench undeniably presented far less daunting construction problems. However, once the anxiety about the growing Japanese aggressiveness had become an imperative with the attack on Pearl Harbor, this route was abandoned in favor of the Northwest Staging Route with its functioning airports available for support.

Bruce McAllister (R), and Brian Fagerlund in McAllister's 1980 Cessna T210 aircraft, flying the Trench, June 2000.

Refueling Bruce McAllister's Cessna 182 at Ingenika during his first trip through the Trench in 1978.

When Bruce McAllister first flew the Trench in a Cessna 182 on a photographic assignment, his concern was about encountering bad weather without sufficient fuel to turn around after the point of no return. Fortunately, he found a seasonal, 6,000-foot (1 830-m) gravel strip at Ingenika at the north end of Williston Lake where he was able to top off his tanks on his way north.

For this trip to Alaska, Post...was operating what is described as a hybrid: the fuselage of a Lockheed Orion, the wings of an experimental Explorer and a set of floats from a Fokker Trimotor. This combination was evidently very unstable...

The Trench featured in an historic flight in 1935. Two world-famous celebrities, pilot Wiley Post and cowboy humorist Will Rogers—renowned for his homespun aphorisms—were on what appears to have been almost a recreational trip to Alaska: territory that Rogers had never seen. Among other things, Rogers wanted to interview an old-timer in Barrow for his newspaper column. Wiley Post, who had lost an eye in an oilfield accident and whose eyepatch gave him a touch of the buccaneer look, had established his fame in 1931 with his

Will Rogers (left) and Wiley Post at Seattle before their departure for Fairbanks on August 16, 1935.
–AP/WIDE WORLD PHOTOS

first round-the-world flight in his Lockheed Vega, the *Winnie Mae*, with Harold Gatty as naviga-

tor. To cap that, he followed up with a solo record-breaking round-the-world flight in 1933.

For this trip to Alaska, Post had retired the *Winnie Mae* and was operating what is described

as a hybrid: the fuselage of a Lockheed Orion, the wings of an experimental Explorer and a set

Two views of the most rugged part of the northern segment of the Trench, 1985. There are few airstrips in this area and most are known only to local guides.

Marginal VFR (visual flight rules) near the north-west end of the Trench in the summer of 1985.

Will Rogers (left) and Wiley Post at Fairbanks during the last stop on their ill-fated flight to Point Barrow. –AP/WIDE WORLD PHOTOS

of floats from a Fokker Trimotor. This combination was evidently very unstable, but Post and Rogers took off from Seattle in August 1935. Stopping at Fairbanks, they left for Barrow in bad weather. Through a break in the cloud cover, they landed on a lagoon 15 miles (24 km) south of Barrow and obtained directions to Barrow from an Eskimo named Opeaha. Shortly

after taking off again, the engine died and the plane dived into a shallow lagoon and flipped over. Both Post and Rogers were killed. Opeaha, "ran all the way to Barrow [about 11 miles (18 km) [over the tundra] to tell of the 'broken bird' and the Signal Corps station radioed news to a shocked world."[14] A well-known Alaska bush pilot, Joe Crosson, flew out to return the bodies to Fairbanks and brought with him photographs of the crash scene.

Now came a race to get the photographs of the crash scene down south for publication in the newspapers. Bush pilot Chet Brown had flown Alfred Lomen and the photographer from Nome to the crash scene. Lomen had also been given the International News Service assignment to get the photographs down to Seattle and he hired pilot Noel Wien to fly them there. The race was between two wire services, Associated Press and International News Service. It was also a race between two pilots and two aircraft: between Noel Wien's Bellanca and Pan American Airways' Fairchild 71. The Fairchild, flown by Harold Holden, was to fly what was considered the normal route from Fairbanks to Seattle: southeast to Skagway and down Lynn Canal to Juneau. Here he would transfer the films to a speedier Lockheed Vega, which would follow the coast to Seattle. Wien decided to take the most direct and potentially dangerous route to Seattle, at night by way of Whitehorse and the Trench.

Undeveloped negatives of the fatal Wiley Post-Will Rogers crash at Point Barrow, Alaska, being transferred for the second time—the first was at Juneau—to be flown to San Francisco. The total trip from Barrow to San Francisco was 42 hours. Pilot Bob Ellis (middle) is handing the package to Seattle bureau personnel. The INS plane, which flew the Trench, beat this aircraft to Seattle.
–AP/WIDE WORLD PHOTOS

An eye-catching view of mineralized lakes just north of Tsay Keh, in the central part of the Trench.

55

The wreck of Post and Rogers' Lockheed Orion just south of Point Barrow, Alaska. Both were killed in this accident.
–AP/WIDE WORLD PHOTOS

Unknown to Wien, Holden, after refueling at Burwash, on Kluane Lake, Yukon, had set off for Haines and Juneau but was turned back by bad weather in the Chilkoot Pass—and then waited it out for several hours in Burwash. Wien, after refueling, took off again from Whitehorse, albeit reluctantly because there was no moonlight. Ironically, the PAA manager in Whitehorse, knowing nothing about his company's entry into the race, offered to drive to the end of the short, 2,000-foot (610-m) strip, and turn on his car headlights to help Wien line up with the runway and see where it ended. The take-off was successful but the navigation tricky. Fortunately, there was just enough light for Wien to pick up landmarks and fly the Trench to Prince George. Within 20 hours of his departure from Fairbanks, Wien landed at Boeing Field in

Billy Phillips

Box 576

Conchas Dam , New Mexico

Seattle at 12:30 pm the next day. On that spectacular flight, passenger/journalist Alfred Lomen

had to wobble-pump extra fuel from five-gallon cans from the plane's cabin into the main tanks.

The competition did not arrive until later that afternoon. By then, INS had a scoop: its

photos of the wrecked aircraft and of Post and Rogers posing beside it before taking off from

Fairbanks were on the street in the Seattle *Post-Intelligencer* before the PAA Vega had landed,

and the Barrow crash was one of the top stories of the year. The route Wien took was an

aviation first. He had pioneered a direct route to Seattle, thereby avoiding the often difficult

weather encountered on the coastal route, and accomplished it in a total flying time of 14

hours and 10 minutes.[15]

**The Rogers-Post funeral plane arriving at Los
Angeles, California on August 19, 1935**
—AP/WIDE WORLD PHOTOS

**First day issue letter commemorating the
cruise to establish the Will Rogers-Wiley Post
Historical Marker, Point Barrow, Alaska,
August 15, 1938.**
—BRUCE MCALLISTER COLLECTION

CHAPTER 4

Flying
The
Highway

Winter twilight on the Alaska Highway near Ft. Nelson. Short winter days make long flights more difficult in the North Country.
–© RICHARD OLSENIUS, 2000

Many thousands of aircraft have flown the Alaska Highway, principally because it is a visual guide; secondly because of the availability of airports and emergency strips along it, and sometimes even to land on it when weather or fuel miscalculations intervene. Of course, the earliest pilots to fly the route had no such visual aid, and even after the completion of the barebones military highway late in November 1942 it did not provide much of a guide. Apparently two years later it was still not easy to follow. Warrant Officer Al Snyder of New Hampshire was one of the ferry pilots taking Lend-Lease Bell P-63s (Kingcobras) up the highway to

World War II portrait of Al Snyder.

—Courtesy Al Snyder

Paula and Don Lounsbury with their Bellanca Scout and Suburban.

—Courtesy Paula and Don Lounsbury

Fairbanks. He recalls that "I could hardly see the Alcan on the way up. We flew the radio beacons a few miles off the Highway and, with a 408–mph [655-km/h] P-63 with the Allison 1500 engines, the plane flew so fast that I could hardly see much on the ground. The Alcan was just a small line through the wilderness."[16]

There were, inevitably (and apart from the Million-Dollar Valley episode), many stories of pilots going astray as well as suffering other mishaps. Nevertheless, over the years many private pilots in light aircraft have followed the highway. It is an adventure even today: a test of fortitude and ability. The problem is that it is very time-consuming, even with a fast light aircraft. Paula and Don Lounsbury had the time but not a particularly fast aircraft: a Bellanca Scout. For several years they had been yearning to fly the highway. Husband Don's sales pitch sounded tempting: "We could fly together enjoying the spectacular scenery and camp under the wing... It would be a great experience!"

"Well, it sounded appealing," Paula reflected, "until he got to the 'camp under the wing' part and then bells started ringing as I recalled past experiences that were anything but great. I began to picture the small, quiet airports my husband was trying to paint as friendly oases: rundown, deserted strips located miles from civilization. No car, no food, no washrooms to be found, only legions of mosquitoes."

They found the solution. They were both pilots, so they decided to tow a travel trailer behind their Suburban. Equipping the truck as well as the aircraft with GPS (Global Positioning System) and radio, they could rotate between legs, one flying while the other drove. The system worked well. The pilot would give the driver an hour's lead time, and they managed to

keep in touch nearly all the time. Starting out from Ontario in May 1998, they crossed the border into the US, flew west and then north, reaching Dawson Creek about two weeks later.

One more sample from Paula's subsequent article about the trip exemplifies the whole experience:

> The following morning brought sunny skies and calm winds…. It was my turn to fly and I was more than just a little nervous at the prospect of flying the next leg to Liard River. The Alaska Highway was located in the narrow valley of the Toad River which proceeded in a westerly direction until it reached the north-south valley where the road turned north towards Muncho Lake.
>
> The mountains rose steeply out of the crystal blue water of the lake to heights of 7,000 to 8,000 feet [2 100 – 2 400 m]. These weren't high peaks by Rocky Mountain standards but it was incredible for this resident of the flatlands of Ontario to be flying at eye level to these giant, jagged ridges. I didn't want to stray too far from the reassuring strip of pavement because there didn't appear to be any other place to land. I felt relief approaching the Liard River valley because it was much wider and seemed more hospitable.[17]

In short, flying or driving the Alaska Highway is still a memorable adventure. Some choose to make it even more challenging.

Shortly after the war ended, in 1946, two young women, Celia Hunter and Virginia Hill,

both of whom were experienced pilots—ex-wartime US Women's Airforce Service pilots

(WASP), attached to the Ferrying Division of the Air Transport Command—decided to make

a winter flight along the highway from Edmonton to Fairbanks. Asked if she had encountered

any male chauvinism as a ferry pilot, Hunter answered "No, the only prejudice was from the

wives of male pilots." On this trip, Hunter was piloting a four-place Gullwing Stinson and her

companion, a two-place Stinson L-5.

They were to be accompanied by two men in a twin-engined aircraft: bush pilot Gene

In July of 1920 five members of the US Army's Black Wolf Squadron pose in front of one of their four de Havilland 4B biplanes in which they flew from Long Island, New York to the Nome, a distance of 4,320 miles. (6 950 km) and logged 55 hours and 50 minutes. The return trip was no less arduous. General Billy Mitchell had authorized the trip to keep his pilots sharp and give them experience in long range navigation. They were led by Captain St. Clair Streett.
— USAAF Photo

I recall sitting on the wing of the Gullwing Stinson at Watson Lake, in minus 30 degrees [F] temperatures with a stiff wind blowing, freezing my hands hanging onto the ice-cold gas cans.

In 1942 Celia Hunter removes a tie-down from a Gullwing Stinson before setting off down the Highway.
—K. Kennedy Collection, 91-098-1143, Archives, University of Alaska, Fairbanks

In the cockpit of a P-47 Thunderbolt fighter, Celia Hunter just before she flew the Alaska Highway in her Gullwing Stinson in December, 1946.
—K. Kennedy Collection, 91-098-1145A, University of Alaska, Fairbanks

Jack, "who learned to fly on the Seward Peninsula in Deering at a mining operation; and Les Edwards, an aircraft mechanic." As it turned out, Jack decided to fly IFR,[18] "over the clouds of an incoming storm, bypassing Dawson Creek to land at Fort St. John, and we didn't see them again until we got to Fairbanks." Before then, however, "they had bought a plumber's firepot—a pressurized gasoline stove for heating plumbing equipment—and put it in my airplane, with no instructions save that we should throw the canvas engine cover over the

engine, light the firepot, stick it under the cover below the nose of the plane and let it stay there until the oil in the engine was thawed enough so the prop could be pulled through.

"We followed these instructions in Dawson Creek, where it was minus 30 degrees [F] the morning we hoped to depart." The firepot lit okay in the heat of the hangar. But when they took it outside and tried to insert it under the hood it flared up and threatened to ignite canvas and plane. "After several tries we took it up town in Dawson Creek, located a plumber, who

Celia Hunter operating the balky firepot at Dawson Creek to start her Gullwing Stinson. The firepot behaved itself after a plumbing supplies expert had adjusted its carburetor.
–K. Kennedy Collection, 91-098-1144, Archives, University of Alaska, Fairbanks

checked it out, discovered it was set for Seattle temperatures, adjusted the carburetor and thereafter it worked okay.

"We had to gas our own planes out of 5-gallon cans at many of the remote airstrips we used. I do recall sitting on the wing of the Gullwing Stinson at Watson Lake, in minus 30 degrees [F] temperatures with a stiff wind blowing, freezing my hands hanging onto the ice-cold cans and pouring the contents into the funnel—very tedious operation.

"On our longest hop—between Teslin and Whitehorse, Ginny [Virginia] had to use the wobble pump to force gasoline out of the spare tank on the back seat of the L-5 into the wing tank—from which it promptly returned to the spare tank because the mechanics had forgotten to install a check valve; so she had to move her wrist back and forth the whole of the rest of the way to keep the plane in the air. Landing ahead of her at Whitehorse, I waited in the terminal for her to crawl out of her plane, but she didn't appear. I finally went down and discovered that she was so tired and cold she couldn't handle the effort of getting out on her own—so I hauled her out and walked her into the terminal where she finally thawed out.

"One humorous incident was when we attempted to land at Big Delta airstrip, on what is now Ft. Greeley. The tower kept giving us an urgent warning but it was cut up by static. We continued to try and land and discovered why he was excited—several huge unyielding bison cluttered up the landing strip."[19]

Celia Hunter (left) and Virginia Hill still live in Fairbanks and are active in the community.
—© MICHAEL MATHERS

67

Paul Bachinger, Suzi Groom and their Luscombe.

In 1972, a young Alaskan couple decided to take up the midwinter challenge, in the opposite direction, in an even lighter aircraft. Paul Bachinger and his fiancée, Susan Groom, flying an 85-hp Luscombe, with no radio, took off from Kodiak on January 14. They landed at Kenai to call Anchorage for permission to land there NORDO (no radio), and arrived there in

After one more scare—a sharp pull up over a telephone line across the road—he made a safe landing and pulled into the driveway of a house.

virtual darkness at 3:15 pm. The Luscombe went into a hangar to be winterized—a new generator and 20-weight oil, among other things—and they set off up the road to join the Alaska Highway at Tok, Mile 1,317 [2 120 km] on the highway, landing at Gulkana to refuel and install the cowling covers in the lower temperatures inland.

On this last leg, Paul had noticed "a rather high oil consumption, but decided the rapid changes in oil temperature might have caused it." Approaching Tok, Paul became aware of two unnerving facts: his oil pressure was down to virtually nil, and his chart indicated that the strip at Tok was not plowed. He tried to divert to another airport on the chart, Tanacross, five miles

Paul Bachinger's Luscombe parked in plumber's driveway after emergency highway landing near Tok, Alaska.
—Courtesy Paul Bachinger

Paul Bachinger pre-heating his Luscombe with stovepipe contraption after emergency landing in Tok, Alaska.

(8 km) away. When they reached it, there were no lights anywhere. "The oil pressure needle was still quivering on zero...my only remaining choice was the longest 'runway' in the world, the Alaska Highway." After one more scare—a sharp pull up over a telephone line across the road—he made a safe landing and pulled into the driveway of a house. It was a plumber's house, and when the plumber arrived home that night, he was convinced he'd had too much to drink.

The next morning, with the temperature at 47 below, they hiked into Tok to purchase oil, which took all day. The following morning was a little warmer but, with a blowtorch and length of stovepipe, it took an hour to get enough heat to the engine for a start at 30 below [F]. When they did, they found that the oil was leaking from the generator seal. They decided the oil would last long enough to reach Northway, at Mile 1,264 [2 034 km] of the highway. There, with the Luscombe in a heated hangar, "we eventually discovered the cause of our trouble: the generator gasket was installed upside down."

Stopping to refuel at Burwash, on Kluane Lake, just east of the Alaska-Yukon border, they pressed on to Whitehorse. The following day, they reached Watson Lake and hoped to carry on to Fort Nelson. But a time change between the two meant not enough daylight; instead they decided to land at the Smith River strip, which was kept cleared, and which boasted a weather station. After a comfortable night there, they were told that Summit Pass, "at 4,218 feet [1 285 m] above sea level the highest point on the Alaska Highway, and the only real bottleneck, was closed in. Coming up on the Summit, things were getting tight. The overcast was right against the pass on the other side and it started snowing heavily. We had to drop down lower and lower and were literally jumping from rock to rock, hoping to find a way through, hugging one side of the canyon in order to be able to turn around any time. Turbulence was picking up, and my passenger was getting quieter and quieter, while I was working hard with the controls and fighting downdrafts. We thought it would never end, but then we broke out of the pass on the other side, where there was a deep drop-off. I pushed hard on the stick to get under the overcast, and there was no more problem." The pass successfully vanquished, they enjoyed a relatively tranquil flight to Fort Nelson, where they "spotted the 6,000-foot [1 800-m] runway. It was as though we were still following the highway. We touched down on the last 1,000

A few minutes later, at a bare 1,000 feet [310 m] the engine stopped dead, without a warning, without a sputter.

Paul Bachinger's Luscombe ready for take-off on Alaska Highway near Tok, Alaska, after emergency landing two days before.
–Courtesy Paul Bachinger

In late September of 1946, near Whitehorse, the Alaska Highway was just a dusty streak across the rugged landscape.
–AP/WIDE WORLD PHOTOS

feet of it and pulled in next to an Air Canada 727."

Held by weather, they took off for Dawson Creek two days later, where they encountered ice fog but found the airport just out of the fog on the outskirts of town. That night, the temperature dropped to minus 51 (F). The following day, the fog still prevailed but the sun could be seen and they took off, "aiming at the sun and hoping to hold her straight until we lifted out of the fog.... We broke out into clear skies and turned right for the road. A few minutes later, at a bare 1,000 feet [310 m] the engine stopped dead, without a warning, without a sputter." Paul made his second, this time dead-stick, landing on the highway. In Alaska, a mechanic had advised him to fly with carburetor heat all the time in cold temperatures. After parking the Luscombe off the side of the road, Paul recalled that the take-off with carb heat on had been unusually long and laboured as had the climb up through the fog. The weather forecast that morning indicated a dew point of minus 10 degrees (F). He concluded that the combination of a really low temperature and the carb heat brought things "close to the dew point, creating conditions perfect for icing. I climbed back into the plane and started up again. Sure enough, she ran like a charm!" He asked a passing motorist to run down the road for a few hundred yards and hold any traffic until he had taken off. "Not until we had reached about 2,000 feet [600 m] did we spot them, at least four miles down the road. We rocked wings in salute and had a good laugh."

Paul and Susan flew on down through British Columbia, Montana and Nevada to their final destination, Lake Tahoe, California, where they landed almost exactly a month after they had left Kodiak. It was a remarkable demonstration of competent airmanship by any standards.[20]

Dawson Creek

M ile zero. Before the Alaska Highway was built, Dawson Creek was a sleepy town of over 500 brave souls farming the land. As a terminus of Northern Alberta Railways, it was the logical staging point for the highway to begin. Inevitably, the start of construction brought with it huge changes: the influx of thousands of US troops and civilian construction workers, many of whom would move on out to start the survey and construction, but all of whom had to be temporarily housed and fed. By the spring of 1942 Dawson Creek had been totally transformed and was no longer a sleepy little agricultural town.

Dawson Creek proudly maintains its modern welcome sign to those about to travel above or on the Highway.
–Courtesy Paula and Don Lounsbury

In the Dawson Creek Control Tower, Ross Donough of Nav Canada using an alidade to measure cloud heights, June 2000.

The opening of the Highway to the general public after the Second World War naturally brought with it an increase in population of hitherto very small communities and a corresponding increase in aviation activity. In Dawson Creek, for example, a small but vigorous group of individuals decided to take to bush flying for a living. They were a colorful bunch representing several generations with varied and unusual careers. Seventy-five-year-old Sam Side flew RAF Lancasters over Germany during the Second World War. By war's end he had completed two tours of duty. He took his commercial check ride with Ernie Boffa, another well-known Canadian pilot, in 1942.

After the war, Sam started a charter service with Bill Whitely and Doug Todd. They chartered for trappers and fishermen and had a flight training school. To improve payload, their Piper J-3 Cub functioned without a starter or radio. No tiger at 65 horsepower, it enabled them to establish a business. They had to take risks early on. Once, in their PA-12 they flew dynamite and caps together to Norman Wells for $500, now prohibited by current regulations.

With the energy boom in British Columbia, Sam could not afford to ignore the oil companies. They paid well, but they wanted to fly regardless of the weather. As Sam puts it, "They wanted charters when it was forty below and wanted to go."[21]

Another local bush pilot, Don Lumsden, moved to Dawson Creek in 1972, also flying in the charter business. Nowadays, he flies a classic Avenger with a 1,950-horsepower Wright R2600 engine. For some time he used it for crop dusting, but now uses a more economical AgCat. Some years ago he flew DC-7s in Senegal, spraying locusts from near treetop level. On his way to Morocco, in company with another DC-7, Saharan dissidents fired heat-seeking missiles that hit both aircraft. The other DC-7, the one that Don had been flying regularly, went down with no survivors. The one that Don just happened to be flying that day dead-sticked to an airstrip. It was an ugly experience for him. The missile hit his No. 1 engine, severing the controls, and he had a runaway engine that eventually tore out if its mount.

Dawson Creek pilots:
Standing - L to R, **Bob Moore (Ministry of Transport), Sam Side, Floyd Meyer**
Front - L to R, **Bob Trail, Phil Brochu, Carson McTavish, Bill Fresho, Don McGowan, Glen McBurney, 1950.**
—Courtesy of Sam Side.

They had to take risks early on. Once, in their PA-12 they flew dynamite and caps together to Norman Wells for $500.

Sam Side (left), and Don Lumsden, with Don's Avenger, at Dawson Creek Airport, June 2000.

Yet another local pilot, Bob Trail, began his flying career in 1948. His instructor was Sam Side and, in the J-3 Cub, they often hovered like a helicopter in strong winds. He observed that in his early days "planes were like cars or pickup trucks because there were practically no roads off the Highway in British Columbia."[22]

While never heavily involved as a major player in the Northwest Staging Route (because the early rush of US military aircraft both to Alaska and Siberia bypassed it), Dawson Creek does have an airport to compete with that of its northern neighbor, Fort St. John. There has always been intense rivalry between the two for air traffic. Dawson does boast an adjacent lagoon for floatplanes, as a convenience for those passengers and pilots who want to switch types quickly, but Fort St. John has a floatplane base at Charlie Lake on the other side of town, about 15 miles (24 km) from the airport.

A Cessna 185 awaiting ice breakup at Dawson Creek Airport, June 2000.

Bob Trail at Dawson Creek Airport, June 2000.

CHAPTER 6

Fort St. John Airport.

Fort
St. John

Until the middle of the 19th century, fur trading posts were inevitably designated as forts, even though some consisted simply of one log building combining a residence for the trader and a warehouse. This would usually be surrounded by a palisade of logs with a gate as protection against potentially aggressive natives and to keep livestock from wandering. Fort St. John and Fort Nelson were two of the earliest fur trading posts in the west, and the native peoples tended to be more aggressive than elsewhere in the north.

Fort St. John is 45 miles (73 km) northwest of Dawson Creek, and just north of the Peace

Aerial view of Fort St. John, 1942.

River. The first fort was located on the north bank of the river, built by the North West Company in 1805. The Hudson's Bay Company took it over in 1821. During this period, fierce and often violent competition was waged between the two companies. More violence occurred in 1823, when the fort was attacked and destroyed in a native attack. Rebuilt on the south bank of the river, it has been moved a number of times. The present fort, erected in 1925, became the centre of the community, which developed into a city by 1975.

The city, then a small, isolated community, made news in 1934 when a millionaire French industrialist, Charles Bedaux, arrived to pioneer a land route through the Rockies. His expedition consisted of two limousines, five Citröen half-tracks, three river bateaux, dozens of hired cowboys, 130 packhorses and several trucks loaded with such necessities in the bush as champagne, caviar and paté de fois gras.[23] His expedition floundered hopelessly and in the end he had to shoot his horses and drift back to Fort St. John by boat. This failed expedition underlined the difficulties of land transport that were so much a part of the Alaska Highway story.

With route surveys flown by Punch Dickins and Daniel McLean dating back to 1935 and Grant McConachie eagerly pushing forward his vision of a Northwest Staging Route—eventually leading to the Orient—in 1938, Fort St. John became a key link in this route. Jack Moar, operations manager for McConachie's Yukon Southern Air Transport started picking out potential landing spots for emergency landing strips along the route.

By 1939, McConachie—whose reputation for persuasive charm became legendary—had convinced locals that airport improvements in Fort St. John would be to their own advantage. At the same time, the deteriorating international situation prompted a renewed interest in the airfields that would ultimately define the Alaska Highway. In 1940, Canadian government crews moved in and started building runways and installing the associated radio and lighting required for round-the-clock aviation movements.

One of the most colorful of bush pilots operating in the Fort St. John area during the postwar era was Jimmy Anderson, a hunting guide based at the tiny community of Pink Mountain at Mile 147. He appears to have flown on a private license. Shirlee Smith Matheson, in her book *Flying the Frontiers*, introduces him with a flourish: "So how did this prairie boy learn the rugged rock piles of British Columbia so intimately that he could land his Super Cub on mountaintops, gravel bars, in the lofty spires of spruce trees—hence the name given both him and his plane: 'Jackpine Savage'—and even in nightmare spots like a river in a box canyon at midnight, winning him his other nickname of 'Midnight.'"

Some of his self-described exploits have to be accepted with a pinch of salt; nonetheless,

"Midnight" Jimmy Anderson's crew at the closest landing strip to the summit of Maternity Mountain, from which they moved the heavy equipment up to the trapping area with the tracked vehicle. Note the live caribou behind the seat of the Piper Super Cub.
—J.F. ANDERSON COLLECTION

Floatplanes at Charlie Lake, Fort St. John area. Public Road Administration's Bellanca and an Army Norseman await missions, 1942.
—GLENBOW ARCHIVES, CALGARY, AB, NA-1796-10

Some of Anderson's sheep herders still in their camouflage white after they had made the first live capture near the summit of Maternity Mountain.

—J.F. ANDERSON COLLECTION

he appears to have achieved some remarkable results operating a Piper Super Cub on oversize tires into and out of unprepared landing sites. Perhaps inevitably, he also suffered "16 crashes. And they weren't even crashes in Anderson's book. It was, well, another 'uncontrolled landing.'"[24] In the end, Midnight Jimmy went through five Super Cubs and evidently (apart from a cut on his nose after it collided with a mounted compass on one of his "uncontrolled landings"), he never suffered injury.

One of his ventures was to capture Stone sheep and caribou for Al Oeming's Alberta Game Farm near Edmonton, Alberta. With the help of several men, he prepared a landing strip as well as a trap on a plateau fairly high in the mountains. Son Jamie, in his book *Outlaw Pilot*, describes how this was accomplished. "Dad's plan was to go to a high flat peak, and set the nets up in a V-shape, with a rope stretched across the opening. Hanging lariat nooses would be attached with hay wire to the taut rope, and the ends of the lariats anchored to large rocks. [Anderson would then herd the sheep into this trap with the Super Cub]. When the sheep were herded through the opening of the V, they would be lassoed by the hung nooses."[25] The four helpers, who had been hiding behind rocks, would then rush in and secure the animals. First attempts were a failure because the helpers were insufficiently concealed and spooked the animals. The following day the helpers, dressed in white sheets, were effectively camouflaged, and the first captures were recorded. The sheep or the caribou were then tied up and flown out on the floor behind the seat in the Cub.

Space is limited here, but apart from Shirlee Smith Matheson's book, Anderson's son, Jamie, has written two books about Midnight Jimmy's adventures.[26]

Midnight Jimmy went through five Super Cubs and evidently (apart from a cut on his nose after it collided with a mounted compass on one of his "uncontrolled landings"), he never suffered injury.

"Midnight" Jimmy Anderson, June, 2000.

CHAPTER 7

Fort
Nelson

Later named after Admiral Nelson, the hero of the battle of Trafalgar, the first fort was built, once again by the North West Trading Company in 1805. This proved to be an unhealthy neighborhood for the fur traders. In 1813, the fort was attacked by natives. Eight people, men, women and children, were massacred and the fort was burned, not be opened again until 1865 by the Hudson's Bay Company.[27]

In Fort Nelson, as in Fort St. John, Grant McConachie's Yukon Southern Air Transport played an important part in the development of the town as an airport on the Staging Route. He was still having to use aircraft on floats or skis, depending on the season, to get through to

The old Hudson's Bay Trading Post at Fort Nelson. In the old days there was a dock nearby to refuel floatplanes. Note the outdoor plumbing at the rear.
–GLENBOW ARCHIVES, CALGARY, AB, NA-1796-28

An aerial photo of the Fort Nelson airport, 1952.

Whitehorse, the largest of them a Ford Trimotor. Here, as in Watson Lake, he had put in a skeleton crew to start construction of an airstrip. With hired native help, they were making progress. By the fall of 1939, they were able to scrape and plow a runway of sorts with packed snow and land their most modern aircraft, a twin-engined Barkley-Grow.

In 1940, a federal government crew moved in and began major airport construction: fields with cleared approaches, 5,000-foot (1 500-m) runways, radio, lighting, and facilities for refueling, maintenance and crew accommodation.[28]

Here once again aerial reconnaissance played an invaluable part in finding the route for the

Meeting place in 1942 of northern and
southern US Army engineers 305 miles west of
Fort Nelson.

—Glenbow Archives, Calgary, AB, NA-1796-15

In 1942, this hill 52 miles west of Fort Nelson
was a real challenge in bad weather. This is in
the Steamboat Mt. Area.

—Glenbow Archives, Calgary, AB, NA-1796-27

Parapup, trained by Lt. David Irwin, worked for the Second Search and Rescue Unit. Many ferry aircraft went down in the Ft. Nelson area—often because of unpredictable weather; sometimes because the air crews did not have much experience.
–Glenbow Archives, Calgary, AB, NA-1845-2

Downed US aircraft near Ft. Nelson in 1943.
–Glenbow Archives, Calgary, AB, NA-1845-1

highway to Watson Lake. Though there was a difficult trail called the McCusker Trail, pioneered in 1890, General Hoge, the military equivalent of a project manager for the highway, concluded that this route would not be feasible. He loaned his twin-engined Beech 18 aircraft to a Major Welling to prospect a new route by way of the Liard River. Bad weather forced the aircraft to try the route both from Fort Nelson and from Watson Lake. He asked the advice of a native in

Watson Lake. The native agreed with the theory that the Liard route would work. There was only one major problem, a steep cliff to navigate at Muncho Lake, one that created some engineering and construction headaches but was eventually overcome.[29]

As with all the major Staging Route posts along the highway, Fort Nelson underwent a dramatic transformation when the American military and the civilian contractors arrived in 1942. An enduring problem for the troops was a chronic shortage of housing. Shortly after the war ended, Sergeant John Piety, who had fallen in love with a Canadian woman, had first to find non-military accommodation before he could gain permission to get married. The problem was eventually solved by the purchase for $300 of a surplus shed that had been used for the

A US B-29 bomber on the ramp at Fort Nelson. This behemoth aircraft looked out of scale at some of the smaller Alaska Highway airports it stopped at for refueling.
—Courtesy Earl L. Brown

A P-51 Fighter at Fort Nelson Airport.
—COURTESY EARL L. BROWN

storage of oil and lubricants. Mounted on a sled, it had been dragged down to a clearing where several other couples had resorted to similar accommodations. A newspaper clipping recorded the marriage of "Miss Josie Bailey and Sergeant J.E. Piety.... Sgt. and Mrs. Piety now live at Teeterville," presumably so named because the sheds literally teetered on their sleds.

Evidently, it was a spartan beginning to their married life. They had no electricity and water had to be carried from a nearby stream. Lighting was by kerosene lanterns and their toilet was a log in the bush. Cooking facilities were similarly primitive; yet they do not appear to look back on it with any sense of dismay. For young love, it was apparently an adventure.[30]

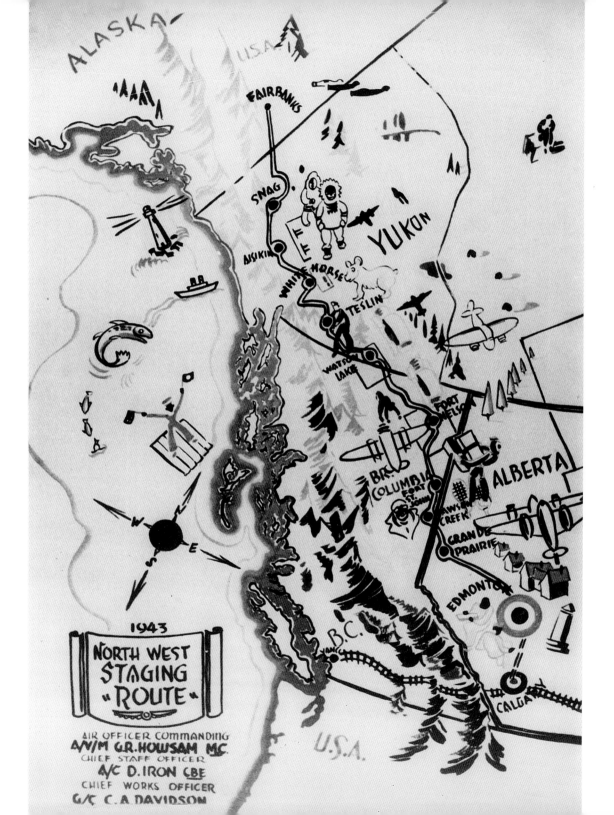

1943
NORTH WEST STAGING "ROUTE"

AIR OFFICER COMMANDING
A/V/M G.R. HOWSAM MC
CHIEF STAFF OFFICER
A/C D. IRON CBE
CHIEF WORKS OFFICER
G/C C.A. DAVIDSON

—Courtesy of Commonwealth Training
Museum, Manitoba

A C-119 Boxcar aircraft engine on display at the Fort Nelson Museum.

—Courtesy Earl L. Brown

A C-119 Flying Boxcar at Fort Nelson Airport.

—Courtesy Earl L. Brown

CHAPTER 8

Watson Lake Airport.

Watson Lake

This lake was named for an Englishman, Frank Watson, who tried to reach Dawson City during the Klondike gold rush by the notorious overland route from Edmonton. He gave up at the lake and settled there to become a trapper. He had lived there ever since, and partnered Jack Baker in McConachie's early attempts to establish an airport.

This was one of the most difficult sites to reach before construction of a fully serviceable airport could begin. Fort Nelson was tough, but eventually reached by bulldozing a trail from Fort St. John, then following up with tractor-trains during the winter. For Watson Lake, on the other hand, it was a long, arduous route: by sea to Wrangell, Alaska, up the Stikine River

Watson Lake Airport in the middle of a typical winter.

—Courtesy Commonwealth Training Museum, Manitoba

Murray Biggin, an avid aviation historian, with the instrument panel from P-39 fighter that went down near Watson Lake because of engine failure. Murray is a bus driver in Whitehorse and also an active pilot.

—© Richard Hartmier

Joe Louis and Canadian officers visiting Watson Lake Airport during World War II.

—Courtesy Commonwealth Training Museum, Manitoba

This de Havilland Beaver, CF-IBP, flew out of Watson Lake for several years and was featured in a book, *Flight of the Red Beaver*, by Larry Whitesitt. In this shot it is shown on the South Nahanni River in Deadman's Valley, Northwest Territories.

—Courtesy Larry Whitesitt

G. M. Kimpinski, CARS Observer Communicator at Watson Lake, is a welcome sight after a long flight. He is more than just a weather man to pilots going up the Alaska Highway for the first time. Legs north and south are long and pilot reports become important.

The first large wartime hangar built on the Alaska highway still stands today at Watson Lake. June, 2000.

by riverboat to Glenora (just south of Telegraph Creek), along a crude trail to the head of Dease Lake, then by scows lashed to riverboats down the Dease River to Lower Post at its junction with the Liard River, and a final 20-odd miles (32 km) overland to Watson Lake.

On the plus side the site itself was an ideal one: a promontory extending out into the lake. It was, moreover, given the limited range of aircraft in the late 1930s, an essential airport for

The terminal building and control tower today, looking much the same as it did during World War II.

Watson Lake terminal building and control tower during World War II.
—Courtesy Commonwealth Training Museum, Manitoba

The Watson Lake Sign Forest, started by a GI in World War II, grows every year and is a must for every tourist.

refueling on the Northwest Staging Route. A considerable proportion of the loads carried down the Dease River consisted of fuel for the heavy equipment to construct it, and avgas for the aircraft about to use it. The log airport terminal goes back to the early '40s and has been designated an historic building.

To this day, the remains of a bomber rest on the south shore of Watson Lake. Also, rumour has it that three locals found a P-38 in the bush, but to save it for posterity and salvage have kept its location a close secret.

Perhaps the most memorable person who ever worked at the airport was a feisty lady named Shirley. She ran the airport café and tolerated no snippiness or insubordination from any pilot. Originally, she was from Inuvik, in the Mackenzie Delta of the Northwest Territories. Her breakfasts were legendary and today it's sad to see only candy and pop machines there.

Among the most critical airports on the Alaska Highway during the Second World War, Watson Lake was picked for the first mega-hangar for servicing transient bombers and fighters. The same hangar still stands, as well as the original control tower.

Remains of a Lancaster bomber are still visible at Watson Lake, across from the north-south runway. The tail is lower center and parts of the fuselage are on shore.

CHAPTER 9

Whitehorse Airport and townsite.
—Courtesy of Geographic Air Survey, Edmonton, Alberta

Whitehorse

A product of the Klondike Gold Rush in 1898, and capital of the Yukon since 1953, Whitehorse is the hub of the whole territory. Its airport has always been a jumping-off point to the interior of the Yukon and its proximity to downtown (on a bluff directly above town) has made it an integral part of Whitehorse. A restored DC-3 dominates the entrance to the airport and the Yukon Transportation Museum there features many famous aircraft and the sister ship to Charles Lindbergh's *Spirit of St. Louis*.

In 1920, four US Army de Havilland DH4B biplanes were the first to fly through the Yukon on the First Alaska Air Expedition. On wheels, they started from Mitchell Field, New York,

114

and succeeded eventually in reaching Nome and returning to New York. It was a brave effort.

Landing strips had to be cleared for them in several locations, including Whitehorse, where

Mike Cyr used a hand saw for the purpose. This primitive strip is part of the airport today.

In October 1927, the first commercial aircraft made its appearance in Whitehorse.

Christened the *Queen of the Yukon*, it was a Ryan M-2 monoplane, sister ship to Lindbergh's

United Air Transport's Fairchild FC-2W2 being refueled for trip to Pelly River in 1932 during a brief gold rush.
—Glenbow Archives, Calgary, NA 3009-3

This DC-3 is right in place at the entrance to the Whitehorse Airport. In 2000 it had an external refurbishment.
—© Wayne Towriss

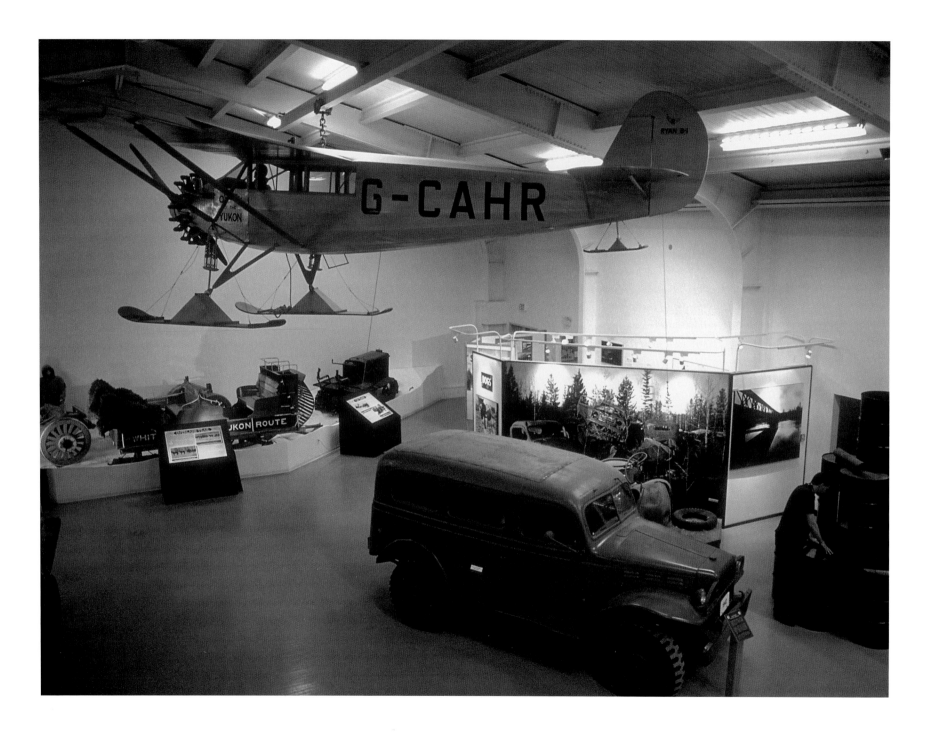

Spirit of St. Louis, and was imported by Andrew Cruickshank, an ex-RCMP officer, and co-founder with businessman Clyde Wann of the Yukon Airways & Exploration Company, another brave venture. In 1927, Cruickshank began to provide airmail service between Whitehorse and Dawson City. Mailbags were air-dropped with varying degrees of accuracy. By 1950, aircraft had finally eliminated sled dogs for mail delivery, making the term air mail a reality throughout the Yukon. That this occurred so late is an indication of the Canadian Post Office

"Queen of the Yukon"—a sister ship to Lindbergh's "Spirit of St. Louis,"—with which Andrew Cruikshank began his air service in Whitehorse in 1927, seen here on display in the Yukon Transportation Museum.

Mailbag used for first official air mail flight between Juneau, Whitehorse, and Fairbanks.
—Bruce McAllister Collection

A Trimotor en route from Carcross to the Pelly River during gold rush in 1932.
—Glenbow Archives, Calgary, AB, NA-3009-2

A group of huskies beside a Northern Airways Fokker Super Universal, CF-AAM. This aircraft was salvaged in the 1980s, was fully restored by aviation enthusiast Clark Seaborn of Calgary Alberta and is presently flying.
—Glenbow Archives, Calgary, AB, NA-2760-5

Department's negative attitude to aviation.

A brave venture it may have been, but unfortunately it was short-lived. Cruickshank found the harsh Yukon winters too much for him. After several mishaps—all of which meant long waits for spares to arrive from the Ryan factory—money ran out and Yukon Airways was dissolved. Andrew Cruickshank went on to a distinguished career as a bush pilot with Canadian Airways until he died in an unsolved accident flying from Great Bear Lake to Fort Rae in the Northwest Territories in June 1932.[31]

Two members of Canada's Aviation Hall of Fame, Grant McConachie and Sheldon Luck, pioneered the first mail runs from Ashcroft, British Columbia, and Edmonton, Alberta, to Whitehorse via Prince George in 1938. A year later McConachie had changed the name of his company from United Air Transport to Yukon Southern Air Transport and won the right to fly mail out of Vancouver. The Vancouver flight would meet the Edmonton one at Prince George and the mail would be transferred to continue north in one or the other of the two aircraft.

First airmail from Edmonton to Whitehorse, signed by Grant McConachie, President of Yukon Southern Air Service, Ltd. 1937.
—Glenbow Archives, Calgary, AB, NA 1120-2

This Barkley-Grow flew into Whitehorse often and was registered to the MacKenzie Air Service until 1941; when this photo was taken it was registered to Canadian Pacific and it was doing a pioneer reconnaissance work between Norman Wells and Whitehorse.
—Yukon Archives, R. Finnie Collection, 81/21-11

A poster, in the Yukon Transportation Museum, advertising services of Northern Airways. This carrier was based in Carcross during World War II.

Whitehorse Airport with a rare view of B-24 bombers and Aircobra fighters on the ramp in October, 1943.
—YUKON ARCHIVES, R. FINNIE COLLECTION, 81/21-445

New hangars under construction at Whitehorse Airport, October, 1943.
—YUKON ARCHIVES, R. FINNIE COLLECTION, 81/21-444

Late in 1939, a Japanese aircraft on a supposed goodwill mission landed at Whitehorse en route to South America. Ironically, a number of US military aircraft passed through Whitehorse that same month, headed north to Alaska. Things were warming up for the Second World War and changing attitudes were beginning to crystallize.

According to the British Yukon Navigation Company's manager of aircraft cargo and passengers at the time, W.D. McBride (who later became the Yukon's most distinguished

Wreck of a military C-47 which crash landed on top of a mountain near Haines Junction, Yukon, in the early 1950s. At the time, this aircraft was on a search and rescue mission, looking for a downed B-25 between Mayo and Whitehorse.

—Courtesy Bob Cameron

historian), running an aircraft operation in the 1940s was somewhat unnerving. "Often a pilot would radio in, 'I'm coming down through the fog' and those would be the last words of that pilot. Later, some pieces of aircraft and bits of mail would be found in Lake Laberge."[32]

In addition to his pioneer survey flying with General Hoge, which determined the route for the highway from Watson Lake to Whitehorse, Les Cook of White Pass Airways earned the US Army's Legion of Merit for a mercy flight in bad weather with two army surgeons to save a man's life. The weather had deteriorated and daylight was fading at the Donjek River landing site, which had to be illuminated by the headlights of every available truck.

Unfortunately Cook was killed when he crashed during a test flight a year or two later.[33]

Downtown Whitehorse in 1944. The station in background was used by White Pass & Yukon Route narrow gauge railway to Skagway.
—NATIONAL ARCHIVES

Grumman-designed and built under license in Canada by De Havilland, S2F fire bombers at the ready on the ramp in Whitehorse. The US Navy used this type for sub hunting.

Russ Baker, another Canadian Aviation Hall of Famer, put in many hours in this area, and was responsible for the rescue of 24 B-26 crew members in the "Million-Dollar Valley" episode—for which he was awarded the United States Air Medal in 1947.

On October 16, 1943, a B-17 ditched in Bennett Lake, 50 miles (80 km) south of Whitehorse. Of the 17 men aboard, only six survived in the icy water. Though the plane was

not severely damaged, it sank quickly into 70 feet (21 m) of water. A Norseman called in to investigate the next day crashed on take-off from Carcross. Divers were eventually called in and the B-17 was barged to the beach, where it could be winched ashore.

This B-17 bomber ditched in Bennett Lake on October 16, 1943. Of the 17 crew aboard, only six survived. The aircraft was winched ashore.
—Yukon Archives, W. J. Preston Collection, 85/ 78-167, 158

Whitehorse Airport at sunrise, June 2000.

Helio Courier making resupply to a glacier research station in the Yukon.
–© Richard Hartmier

Finally, as an essential fuelling stop for all aircraft, large and small, Whitehorse is by far the most important airport on the Alaska Highway, with the best food and lodging to match. As well, with its parallel runways of 4,000' and 7,000' and a shorter one of 2,075' (1 220 m, 2 130 m & 650 m), it can handle most modern airliners.

CHAPTER 10

A color infrared aerial view of Northway airport and surrounding area, 1986.
–USGS/EROS Data Center, Sioux Falls, SD
(Map: AtII 4105 304.97)

Northway

The air base at Northway was an even more difficult site to get to than Watson Lake when construction began in the spring of 1941. Watson Lake was open to bush aircraft year round, but for freeze-up and break-up seasons; whereas Northway had no ready access by air or ground. But it was an important part of the Staging Route because it was halfway between Whitehorse and Fairbanks—a necessary refueling point. It was also the first customs station for pilots heading into Alaska along the highway. Historian Lavell Wilson describes the initial moves:

The Civil Aeronautics Authority (CAA) gave Morrison-Knudsen Co.

(M-K) the contract for construction of the Northway airport and in the spring of 1941, months before the United States entry into the war, well-known bush pilot Bob Reeve flew M-K construction foreman Pat Walker and some tools into Tetlin, the closest landing strip. From there the men went upriver by boat to Northway and, using a Native crew of 20, they built a 100-foot by 800-foot [30 x 245-m] airstrip in six days. Reeve immediately began hauling men and supplies into this tiny airfield. As the closest road ended at the Nabesna Mine, about 50 miles [80 km] upriver from Northway, supplies were trucked to the end of that road and then flown to the construction site. Bob Reeve flew in most of the supplies in his Fairchild 71 and later in a Boeing 80A, dubbed the "Yellow Peril," that M-K ordered from Seattle. Everything was flown in except the large, 17-ton tractors that pulled 12-ton scrapers.[34]

Once again, aircraft led the way and roads came later. The end of the road at the Nabesna Mine was turned into an airstrip and pilots worked in shifts, seven days a week during the long daylight hours of spring and summer: "1,100 tons of supplies and 300 construction workers were flown in…in less than five months." When the Alaska Highway reached Northway a short, seven-mile (11-km) road was pushed in, connecting it with the highway[35] and making Northway a major part of the Northwest Staging Route.

Once again, aircraft led the way and roads came later. Pilots worked in shifts, seven days a week during the long daylight hours of spring and summer

Bob Reeve in front of a Fairchild 51 at Valdez in 1936. He used many types of aircraft to support the Northway airport construction.
—Bob Reeve Collection / Reeve Alaskan Airways, Courtesy of Jim Ruotsala

135

Aerial view of Northway airport in 1943. It was
the toughest airport to build on the Alaska
Highway because of its remoteness.

—Courtesy Don F. Tomlinson

Loading a C-47 aircraft headed for Northway
with construction equipment. Note the
Studebaker truck being loaded in pieces.

—Courtesy Don F. Tomlinson

Bush pilot Merle "Mudhole" Smith who earned his nickname clearing mud out of a radial engine after nosing over on a muddy field.
—Bruce McAllister Collection

"Mudhole" Smith, another well-known Alaska bush pilot, flew freight into Northway during this period and recalled sleeping along the runway one night, dead tired, oblivious to the 24-hour-a-day traffic. Next morning he woke up, confronted by 21 parked DC-3s. Bound for Fairbanks, they had been forced by weather to stop short at Northway. Because of war priority, many still bore Delta and Eastern Airlines' logos; they had been pulled off scheduled runs to move freight and people north.[36]

After the war, Northway was retained and maintained as a well-equipped civil airport.

Morrison-Knudsen Boeing 80A Trimotor had the payload to help move construction materials to build the Northway airport.
—Courtesy Jim Ruotsala

Note large cargo door of Boeing 80A Trimotor.
—Gordon Williams Photo, Courtesy Jim Ruotsala

139

A Morrison-Knudsen Vultee V1-A was a
handful to fly but was very fast. Its Cyclone
engine had a nasty habit of losing oil pressure;
sometimes at critical phases of flight. It was
used in supplying the Northway airport.

—Courtesy Jim Ruotsala

Early winter sunset at Northway airport, 1969.
—Courtesy Paul Bachinger

CHAPTER 11

Fairbanks International Airport.
© Patrick J. Endres

Fairbanks

Ice fog makes Fairbanks one of the trickiest winter destinations for those who fly the Alaska Highway. From the late 1930s to the discovery of oil on the North Slope in 1968, this airport has been the key aviation staging point for Alaska's vast interior.

Noel Wien, Ed Young, Carl Ben Eielson, Joe Crosson, Harold Gillam, Art Woodley and Bob Reeve, the elite of the pioneer bush pilots, did perhaps more than any others to develop aviation in Alaska, particularly in Fairbanks. In 1924, Wien arrived there at the same time as the recession and the gold dredges. He went on to pioneer flights to every corner of Alaska. As its first bush pilot, he pioneered the Anchorage-Fairbanks run; he was the first pilot to fly

Frank Barr, another veteran Alaska bush pilot, started commercial flying in Alaska in the Juneau-Skagway area; he flew for Alaska Air Transport in 1937 and became owner-manager in 1938. He was involved in the construction of the Alaska Highway.

—COURTESY JIM RUOTSALA

Mary Worthylake, who was married at the time to well-known Alaska bush pilot Joe Barrows, was the first woman pilot licensed in Alaska. She earned her wings in mid-1932.

—K. KENNEDY COLLECTION, 82-105-03, ARCHIVES, UNIVERSITY OF ALASKA, FAIRBANKS

Noel Wien (L) and Carl C. Dunbar at Fairbanks, May 23, 1925.

—NOEL WIEN COLLECTION, VFSM-60-959-18, ARCHIVES, UNIVERSITY OF ALASKA, FAIRBANKS

Archie Ferguson, the eccentric and unpredictable Alaska bush pilot who also owned a profitable bush flying outfit. There are numerous quotes attributed to him, one of which went as follows: "A federal inspector once advised him to study meteorology. 'Metrinology,' he snarled back, 'What the hell is that? I never keep no log book,' he told me, 'Just when I crack up, that's all.'"

—Burleigh Putnam Photo

north of the Arctic Circle and land. Then he went on to pioneer commercial flights between Fairbanks and Nome and between Seattle and Fairbanks.

While doing so, Wien developed cold weather techniques for operating in sub-zero temperatures. He was a perfectionist in aircraft maintenance, changing oil every five hours of flight time, and refusing to fly if he felt conditions were not just right for him. In short, he was intelligently cautious about weather and maintenance. He did not smoke, drink or allow his health to deteriorate. More than once he had to walk out of the bush and he was always in condition to do so.

Bob Reeve, a close friend of Wien's, moved to Fairbanks in 1935 and, with their mutual friend, Harold Gillam, they pioneered such things as automatic direction finding (ADF) homing and "blind flying"—or instrument flying—in Alaska. Gillam upset the Signal Corp when his home-based radio station seriously interfered with the Fairbanks radio stations. Reeve delivered a comprehensive variety of supplies and equipment to the mines deep in the interior, and went on to pioneer glacier landings in Alaska.

One of the most unconventional and humorous pilots in the Alaska bush was Archie Ferguson, who flew between Fairbanks and Kotzebue (550 miles [885 km]) northwest of Fairbanks). "The Little Man" had his first plane ride with Noel Wien in 1926. He was rumored to have an income of $200,000 a year from his own air service and pioneered the use of ham radios in the Arctic. Once, while the lend-lease operation was in full swing, he flew into Galena. "Some soldier told me ta call him on the downwind leg o' the beam. I said, 'Where the hell is that?' Oh Christ I must have been right on it. I landed okay but it took me an hour to git

Harold Gillam early in his bush pilot career in 1929. He's in what appears to be an open cockpit Standard.

—Courtesy Jim Ruotsala

Bob Reeve (left) and photographer Russ Dow, 1938. Reeve arrived in Alaska in 1932 and became famous for the glacier landings he pioneered in the Valdez area to carry supplies to the surrounding mines. During the Second World War, under contract to the government, he flew men, equipment and supplies throughout Alaska; including the construction of the Northway airport. In 1980, his Reeve Aleutian Airways served 22 communities, along 2,183 air-route miles.

—K. Kennedy Collection, 91-098-1258, Archives, University of Alaska, Fairbanks

147

A Northern Air Transport Trimotor awaits passengers. The company flew the Valdez-Fairbanks route in the 1930s.

—K. KENNEDY COLLECTION, 91-098-102, ARCHIVES, UNIVERSITY OF ALASKA, FAIRBANKS

Weeks Field, Fairbanks, as it looked from the air in 1934.

—NOEL WIEN COLLECTION, 60-959-6N, ARCHIVES, UNIVERSITY OF ALASKA, FAIRBANKS

Ed Young arrived in Fairbanks in 1925 from San Diego, to fly for Bennett & Rodebaugh. Later he flew for Alaska Airways and was active in the search for Eielson. He flew for Pan American Airways out of Fairbanks until his untimely death in a plane crash at Livengood in the early 1930s. Here he is seen with a passenger beside a Waco 10 at Weeks Field, Fairbanks, in 1929.

ED YOUNG COLLECTION, F/56 81 24 83, ARCHIVES, UNIVERSITY OF ALASKA, FAIRBANKS

PACIFIC ALASKA AIRWAYS

U.S.A
NX
18973

...OUND THE WORLD RECORD FLIGHT
...OWARD HUGHES PLANE.
...RBANKS - JULY 13, 1938

out o' that place. They told me I gotta git the weather. I told 'em 'I don't need no weather; I ain't had no weather all day.'" One airline pilot remarked, "the more I see Archie Ferguson fly, the less I fear an airplane."[37]

In 1938, the celebrated Howard Hughes, who played a significant role in the development of aviation, stopped briefly at Weeks Field on his round the world flight in a twin-engined Lockheed Lodestar. Originally, Hughes had bought a Douglas DC-2 for the trip but changed his mind and flew the faster Lockheed. Money was never an issue for Hughes and he enriched

Winter scene at Ladd Field, Fairbanks. A dog team of the ATC's Alaska Division "mush on" down the line past a C-47 Skytrain (left) and a C-46 Commando. The Commando at the time was the world's largest twin engine transport plane.
—Kennedy Collection, 91-098-840, Archives, University of Alaska, Fairbanks

A C-130 Hercules aircraft unloading a truck during the 1969 discovery of oil on Alaska's North Slope. Only two oil rigs were working in the Arctic when this photo was taken in January of 1969.
—© Bruce McAllister

Pre-heating an Everts Air C-46 Commando at Fairbanks International Airport, which is about to ferry fuel to the Alaska Arctic.
—© Michael Mathers

aviation by both designing and building advanced aircraft. His most spectacular aircraft was the huge flying boat, the Hughes H-4 Hercules (nicknamed the "Spruce Goose"), in which he made a brief but sensational trial run in Los Angeles harbor on November 2, 1947. It was meant to be a taxiing trial, but became a low-level flight for about a mile (1.6 km). As historian Herb Noble comments, "Pratt & Whitney developed a monster engine. Again 'bolting together' they came up with a 28-cylinder four-row radial engine they called the Wasp Major R 4360, developing 3000 horsepower...eight of these engines are on the 'Spruce Goose.'"[38]

For a variety of reasons the "Goose" never flew again, but it has been preserved and recently moved to the Evergreen International Aviation Museum in McMinnville, Oregon, from Long Beach, California.

Since 1940, when the US Army Air Force set up a weather station at Fairbanks, it has been a key military town for both the Army and the Air Force. Fifty percent of Fairbank's employment is through the federal government.

A pilot runs toward an HH-3 Jolly Green Giant helicopter during a search and rescue exercise near Fairbanks in 1990.
—MSGT Fred Botce/USAF

A USAF Search & Rescue Sikorsky H-4 Helicopter accomplishing the first helicopter landing on a glacier in Alaska in 1948.
—© Bradford Washburn, Courtesy Panopticon Gallery, Waltham, MA

Eielson AFB, south of Fairbanks, has over 60,000 square miles of military training airspace and is said to have North America's longest runway— 14,057 feet (4 284 m).

A-10 Thunderbolt II close support aircraft in formation near Fairbanks in 1984. They were assigned to the 18th Tactical Fighter Squadron at Eielson AFB at the time.
—TECH. SGT. LOU HERMANDEZ/USAF

Flares descend over bombing range after being dropped from a 343ʳᵈ Tactical Fighter Wing A-10A Thunderbolt II aircraft during CALFEX'90, a joint service combined arms live-fire exercise.
—MSGT ED BOYCE PHOTO/USAF

Eielson Air Force Base south of Fairbanks has over 2,600 military personnel, with over 4,000 dependents on and off base. The 354th Fighter Wing equips and trains its 18th Fighter Squadron for offensive counter-air, interdiction and close-air support roles. It currently uses the F-16 Fighting Falcon. The wing's 355th Fighter Squadron flies the OA-10 and A-10 Thunderbolt II aircraft in close air support missions. Eielson has over 60,000 square miles of military training airspace and is said to have North America's longest runway–14,057 feet (4 284 m).

The US Army at Fort Wainright (formerly Ladd Field), has over 4,500 soldiers, 1,600 civilians, and over 6,000 dependents. The Army base also assists in search and rescue operations for the region.

A Cessna 180 parked outside a typical Fairbanks home—much like a pickup truck, 1975.

Cliff Everts uses DC-6s, a C-119 and a C-46 to fly fuel to remote villages in the Alaska Arctic.
—© Sam Harrel

Four F-15 Eagle fighter aircraft with Mt. Denali in the background. For many years, this all-weather fighter has been a key part of Alaska's air defense.
—Courtesy McDonnell Douglas Corporation

A US Fish & Wildlife Cessna 185 made an emergency landing on the highway near Fairbanks in 1999. It had a bad fuel valve, giving the pilot use of only one of his two fuel tanks. After adding some fuel to the usable fuel tank, the pilot headed for more normal surroundings!
—© Sam Harrel/Fairbanks News Miner

From the early 1950s, helicopters operated extensively along the Alaska Highway. In the 1980s, this Hughes 500 was working on a mining exploration project in Alaska.

Alyeska Pipeline Patrol helicopter pilot
checking his charts.
—© Bruce McAllister

Alyeska pipe line just north of the Brooks
range as it approached Prudhoe Bay in
October, 1975. At the time it was still under
construction.

The Alyeska Pipeline, north of Fairbanks in Fall
of 1986. Like the Canol Pipeline, it was built
above ground. Special insulators prevented the
pipeline from damaging the permafrost.

Jim Walatka, another of Alaska's celebrated bush pilots in a candid moment, 1965.
–K. Kennedy Collection, 91-098-1295, Archives, University of Alaska, Fairbanks

A color infrared aerial of Fairbanks International Airport, 1986.
–USGS/EROS Data Center, Sioux Falls, SD (Map: 1815 03582 ALK 60 CIR AUG 86)

Fairbanks International Airport is the northernmost and largest airport on the Alaska Highway. It features parallel runways of 10,300 and 3,200 feet (3 140 and 975 m), as well as a 3,980-foot (1 210-m) ski strip and a lagoon for floatplanes. Every week it's a fuel stop for over 30 transpolar wide body cargo flights from Europe to Asia. Six commuter carriers are based at Fairbanks International and serve interior and Arctic communities. And over 500 general aviation aircraft are based in the Fairbanks area.

CHAPTER 12

Howard Smiley, co-pilot of one of the three B-26 bombers that made emergency landings in the Million Dollar Valley. Smiley is with his original B-26, Serial No. 40-1464. Except for its nose and main gear, the bomber has original parts. The nose and gear were salvaged off the other two bombers.

The Million Dollar Valley

The story of the three B-26 Martin Marauder bombers' crash-landings in a wide valley immediately to the east of the Smith River, in British Columbia, and just south of the Yukon border, on January 16, 1942, has been told many times—yet still, 58 years later, new information emerges.

The safest way to avoid a repetition of the hyperbole, not to say purple prose, normally associated with this dramatic episode is to record descriptions by participants. First, we have an account by the co pilot of one of the bombers, Lieutenant Howard F. Smiley, who now lives in Florida and who, in company with many other pilots and navigators, assembled to pick up their brand-new B-26 bombers at the Sacramento Air Depot. They took off to begin their flight to Alaska on January 5, 1942. "[At that time], as co-pilot and observer [in a B-26], I had a total of ten hours, no landings or take-offs. My first pilot, who outranked me by five weeks, was a little better off with a little more time and about two landings and take-offs.".

The first stop in their aircraft was Great Falls, Montana, where the 7th Ferry Group prepared them for the trip to Edmonton, Alberta. They arrived in Edmonton on January 15, and set off for Whitehorse the following day, each bomber with a crew of six:

> On the evening of the 15th, our CO, Major Cork, gathered the pilots into his room for a briefing. Among other things he explained that there were no aeronautical maps to take us beyond Edmonton to Whitehorse, Yukon Territory, our next stop. This was to be a flight of some 1000 miles [1 600 km].
>
> Then Major Cork introduced us to a couple of Canadian bush pilots who, on 8.5" x 11" sheets of paper, had made pencil sketch maps showing a lake here, a river there, etc. This was all very nice of them, but in a run of 1000 miles we were to see actually hundreds of lakes and [several] rivers! They left us with a cheery, "You can't miss it [Whitehorse]".[39]

One thing Smiley's account clearly illustrates is what an admirable job these young and relatively inexperienced crews accomplished in an environment that must have been almost totally alien to most of them.

The Instrument panel of Smiley's bomber.

What we did not realize was that the snow is deeper on the valley floor and what looked like tuffs of grass were actually the tops of bushes sitting in 4' to 5' [1.2 to 1.5 m] of snow.

A view of the snow-covered valley, over the wing of Smiley's downed aircraft.

The Navigator's desk of Smiley's bomber.

Because "each plane was carrying a full crew including a celestial navigator with his sextant," this particular flight of three bombers experienced no difficulty up to and beyond Fort Nelson: "The sun was out and the navigators could take their sun lines." Then "we ran into a snowstorm and had to drop down and try to find our way with pilotage, a tricky thing to do in the Canadian Rockies." Before long the light was fading and they were running out of fuel; so they made the sensible decision to find a "shallow valley and try for a good forced landing. A suitable shallow valley was quickly found and the other two planes bellied in with no injuries."

Smiley recalls that the spot they picked for a landing was quite level "and in the gathering darkness the surface appeared smooth with little tuffs of grass sticking up above the snow. What we did not realize (due to lack of experience in mountain flying and not being briefed in the matter) was that the snow is deeper on the valley floor and what looked like tuffs of grass were actually the tops of bushes sitting in 4' to 5' [1.2 to 1.5 m] of snow." He continues

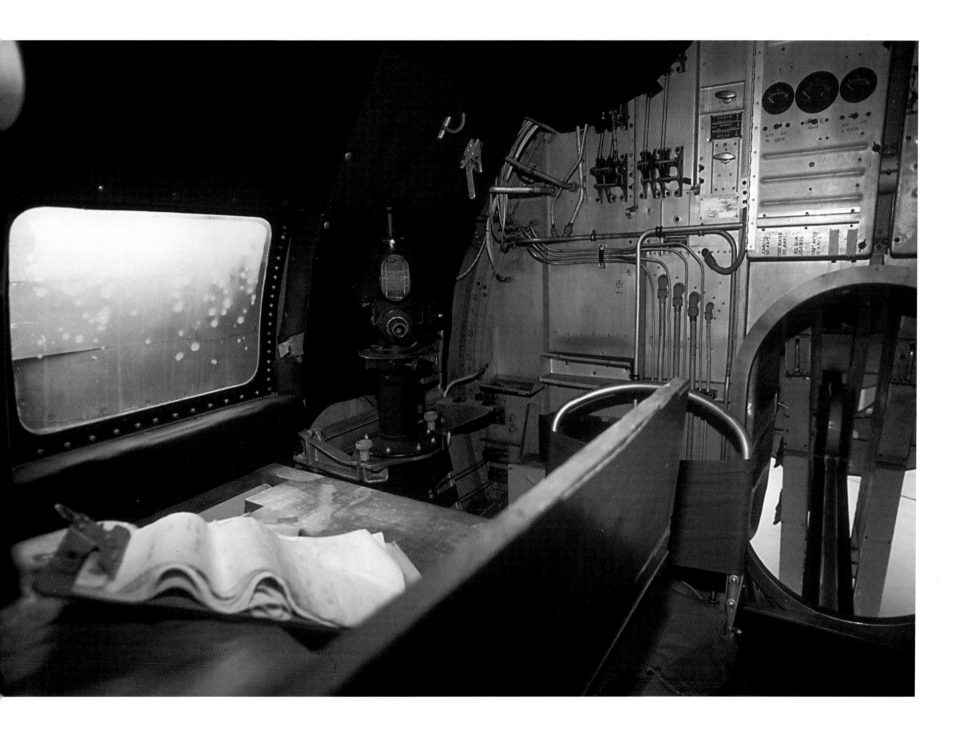

As we hit, the plane swung 90° to the left, the nose wheel collapsed and the nose dug in the ground, popping open like a baked potato.

The severely damaged cockpit of Smiley's B-26 after its wheels-down landing in the snow.
–HOWARD SMILEY COLLECTION

A view of the invitingly wide and flat valley in which the three B-26 pilots chose to land.

his account of the landing:

> It was then our turn. As we were on the final approach, our speed was excessive— we would bring these early speed demons in at about 140-150 mph [225-240 km/h]; they would stall out at about 125 mph [200 km/h]—and so to slow the plane down a bit, Dancer called for wheels and I lowered the landing gear.... As we hit, the plane swung 90° to the

173

Shepard's crew at work on the salvage. The damage to the nose after the crash landing is evident. After 30 years, one tire is still inflated.
—RICHARD SHEPARD/HOWARD SMILEY COLLECTION

The main gear of Smiley's rebuilt bomber was salvaged from one of the other two bombers.

left, the nose wheel collapsed and the nose dug in the ground, popping open like a baked potato. Dancer went out through the windshield with head injuries. I was knocked out in my seat with my feet entangled in the controls. The rest of the crew was in good shape.

Howard Smiley standing beside his damaged B-26, January 17, 1942, before rescue. At the time he was injured and had not yet received medical attention.

—HOWARD SMILEY COLLECTION

SURVIVAL

Fig. 5

After the crew had administered first aid to the two pilots, they "whipped out the wing covers and made a fine shelter under the left wing. Fortunately we had emergency gear which was sufficient for the duration—gear which included arctic type wear, sleeping bags for all and food rations for two weeks, so we settled down for a long stay. Both Dancer and I could get around in good shape."

An illustration from a USAAF Pilot's Survival Manual. This was carried on flights up the Alaska Highway

—Courtesy Sam Side

176

Two days after the landing, January 18, Smiley records that it

dawned clear and cold (about 0°). Along toward noon, as we were in

our cozy shelter, we suddenly heard a low humming noise off in the

distance. We dashed outside and looking toward the sound [south] we

saw several little specks and one larger speck going from left to right

Smiley's aircraft with the emergency wing-cover shelter in which the crew waited for their rescue.
—HOWARD SMILEY COLLECTION

This was one of the B-26s as Richard Shepard and his salvage crew found them in 1972.

—Richard Shepard/Howard Smiley Collection

just over the trees on the horizon. These specks were the P-40Es and their escort on their way from Fort Nelson to Watson Lake. Our crews, as well as the other crews, had prepared for just such an event. Almost immediately, flares and tracer bullets from the planes' guns started to blaze away, a real Fourth of July! We watched to see if the planes had seen our signals. Suddenly the whole flight slowly turned to the right and flew over our positions.... As the planes passed over us, we all stood outside so that they could count us and see that there was no serious injury amongst us.

On the following day, January 19, Smiley records that a single-engine monoplane on skis, with two pilots, landed at the site. "While the two pilots remained with the ship a Canadian Mountie[40] got out to check the condition of the personnel of our three planes and found that only Dancer and I would possibly need a little more medical attention. He loaded us into the skiplane and then returned to the three planes to see what more help he could be to them." Smiley and Dancer were flown to Watson Lake. From there, they were flown by the USAAF to Ladd Field, Fairbanks, Alaska. Two days later Smiley was pronounced fit and a week later he was back flying what he called "our beloved beast, the straight B-26," on his way to the Aleutians.[40]

The second account is by one of the two BC Provincial policemen, Keith Alexander, who was then stationed at the Fort Nelson detachment, and who wrote this official report only a few days after returning there from the rescue. Dated February 5, 1942, the report is addressed to Inspector T. Van Dyk, O.C. "D" Game Division, Prince George, B.C.

> On Saturday morning, January 17th, 1942, while on business at the Fort Nelson Airport, two American Transport Planes and Seven Pursuit Planes arrived at the airport. Lieut. Smith i/c of the flight informed me that he had just received word that three American Bombers of the 77th Medium Bomber Squadron had been lost from a flight of six, the previous day, somewhere between Fort Nelson, B.C. and Watson Lake, Y.T. Same date at 12:15 p.m. the lost bombers were contacted by the radio station at Fort Nelson Airport.... At that time they gave their position south of the Liard River fairly close to Watson Lake....

I suggested that… [if they needed medical equipment or dogs] the Nelson Detachment was at their service.

Same date at 10:00 p.m. Lieuts. Smith and Krebes…stated that they had received the exact location of the three lost bombers…. The position now given was forty miles [65 km] northwest of Nelson Forks in the Beaver River country. Smith asked me if I could accompany them first thing in the morning and bring my medical kit with me….

On Sunday, January 18th, 1942 at 9:30 a.m. I left Fort Nelson Airport with Lieut. Krebes in one of the American Transports. Lieut. Smith left at the same time to convoy the seven Fighters through to Whitehorse, Y.T. At 10:30 a.m. while searching over the Beaver River Country we received a report that Lieut. Smith had spotted the Bombers. We then headed direct to Watson Lake. At 11:30 a.m. we spotted the three Bombers, lying approx. two miles apart at the bottom of a big valley about thirty miles [48 km] south and east of Toobally Lakes, altitude 4000 feet [1 220 m], in a direct line about 90 miles [145 km] east of Watson Lake in British Columbia. We flew low over the Bombers and then in to Watson Lake, arriving there at 12:30 p.m.

Upon arrival at Watson Lake I was met by Major Cork…. Pilot Russ Baker and Game Warden Jack Purdy[42] were also there, having arrived in a Canadian Airways plane, Junkers on skis. At the request of Major

Cork and Pilot Russ Baker, Purdy and I agreed to accompany Russ Baker in the Junkers to the location of the Bombers to see what could be done. Same date at 3:00 p.m. we left Watson.... Upon arrival at the Valley, we flew in circles over a spot near the middle bomber.... Baker stated that he did not feel like landing because daylight was fading. We then flew to Toobally Lakes [some 20 miles (32 km) north of the crash site] to spend the night in a trapper's cabin.

Another view of the wreckage, 1972.
–RICHARD SHEPARD/HOWARD SMILEY COLLECTION

When they had settled in for the night at Toobally Lakes, Russ Baker, the pilot, suggested that, if he couldn't land, he could fly them back to Watson Lake to pick up a dog team to accomplish the rescue. Both Alexander and Purdy advised that it would take at least a week just to get to the site and back with a dog team, and then only "if the fine weather that had never been known in that season," didn't change; and, in any case, they would be able to bring only one man out at a time. When they circled the site again and landed the next morning, Alexander describes the landing as "none too smooth." Next he gives the names of the injured in the southernmost bomber—which landed wheels down—and the extent of their injuries: "We found Lieut. Dancer i/c of that plane with a broken nose and slight internal injuries, Lieut. Smiley with a cut on his head and weak from loss of blood. I pulled the bombsight on one engine cowling, while Purdy pulled Dancer on another….[43]"

While this was being done, Baker put the crew of the nearest bomber to work stamping out a runway for take-off—a standard practice on deep snow—then took off and flew the injured men to Watson Lake.

Alexander and Purdy remained with the middle bomber crew for the night. On the following day, Tuesday, January 20, "Baker made several trips with the bomber crews to Toobally Lakes. On Wednesday…Purdy and myself with the remaining men made another trip to the north ship and on instructions from Major Cork, destroyed secret papers and any injured secret instruments. We then returned to the middle Bomber…and were met by Baker who had just landed and all left for Toobally Lakes. Another Canadian Airways Fairchild on skis came in to the Toobally Lakes and with the Junkers was just able to take the remaining

personnel…to Watson Lake. Purdy and I remained…at the cabin." Alexander and Purdy were picked up and flown to Watson lake the following day.

In summary, it is unfortunate that most journalists ever since found it necessary to elevate the rescue to high drama in the wilderness; embellishing it to the point of ridicule in some cases. Given the wonderful break with the weather (Alexander described it as "the fine weather that had never been known at that season"), it was still an admirably organized and competent operation, carried out with skill and no little courage.

Clark Seaborn flying his restored Fokker Super Universal. He helped salvage the frame, and then spent 17 years rebuilding it virtually from scratch with original blueprints. Less than a month after the bombers went down, a sister ship, CF-AJC, flown by Alec Dame, with pilot-engineer Herman Peterson, flew into the valley to salvage what they could. Several aircraft were involved and they flew out virtually everything, including the engines, leaving only the shells of the fuselages and the wings. Richard Shephard's party removed these in 1972.
—Courtesy Jeffrey Seaborn

Liard River, one of the more dramatic airstrips on the Highway, is still available for emergency use. June 2000.

Secondary Airports and Airstrips

Beatton River

This old airstrip was designated Flight Strip No. 2 in the Second World War and completed in late 1943. Use only north part, because of washout. If wet, do not use!

Sikanni Chief

Limited maintenance for this 6000' (1 830 m) airstrip. In old days also known as **Pink Mountain Strip**. If wet, do not use!

Airstrips of the Alaska Highway, Past and Present.

(In Sequence–From Southeast to Northwest)

Dawson Creek, British Columbia. **CYDQ**

Fort St. John, British Columbia. **CYXJ**

Beatton River, British Columbia.
57° 23'N, 121° 23'W

Sikanni Chief, British Columbia.
57° 05'N, 122° 36'W

Prophet River, British Columbia.
57° 58'N, 122° 47'W

Fort Nelson, British Columbia. **CYYE**

Toad River, British Columbia, Mile 422. **CBK7**

Liard River, British Columbia.
59° 31'N, 126° 22'W

Smith River, British Columbia.
59° 54'N, 126° 26'W

Watson Lake, Yukon. **CYQH**

Pine Lake, Yukon. **CFY5**

Teslin, Yukon. **CYZW**

Squanga Lake, Yukon. **CFR6**

Whitehorse, Yukon. **CYXY**

Champagne, Yukon.
60° 47'N, 136° 29'W

Haines Junction, Yukon. **CYHT**

Aishihik, Yukon.
61° 39'N, 137° 29'W

Silver City, Yukon. **CFQ5**

Burwash, Yukon. **CYDB**

Snag, Yukon.
62° 22'N, 140° 24'W

Beaver Creek, Yukon. **CYXQ**

Northway, Alaska. **PAOR**

Tanacross, Alaska. **TSG**

Fairbanks International Airport, Alaska. **FAI, PAFA**

USE AIRSTRIPS AT YOUR OWN RISK, AND ONLY AFTER CHECKING
WITH LOCAL PILOTS & CARS PERSONNEL

Prophet River,

This 6,000' (1 830 m) airstrip was an emergency airstrip in the Second World War and is still

in use today as a seasonal airstrip. It was known as Flight Strip No. 3.

Toad River

This private airstrip's name predates a Hudson's Bay Trading Company's post that was active

here in the late 1880s. In 1831, explorers noticed that there were numbers of large toads on the riverbanks. Today the airstrip is operated by the Toad River Community Club (250) 232-5401. Stone Mountain Safaris B&B. Ellie & Dave Wiens, operate a full-breakfast B&B and are outfitters (250) 232-5469. There are hot springs north of this tiny settlement. The length 2500' (760 m), listed is considered by local pilots to be a bit inflated. Call ahead for permission to use and runway conditions.

Liard River

Lengthened in the 1990s from 1,400' to some 4,000' (430 to 1 200 m) this is now a seasonal airstrip, relatively user friendly today. Liard is French for a type of poplars that grows along the riverbanks. The local hot springs are popular with today's motorists and were a desirable break for the Army Engineers building the Alaska Highway in 1942. Around 1840, Explorer Robert Campbell is reputed to have been the first white man to pioneer this route into the Yukon. Decades later, many gold-rush Klondikers met their end in this rugged valley. Because it is sandy, it drains well.

Smith River

In the Second World War, this abandoned airstrip, close to the Smith River and just south of the BC-Yukon border, was known as Flight Strip No. 4. Current condition unknown.

Smith River Airstrip, June 2000 This was a
staging airstrip for the recovery of the Million
Dollar Valley B-26s.

Pine Lake Airstrip, June 2000. This is a key emergency airstrip on the Alaska Highway and, in bad weather, the relatively high terrain usually has lower ceilings.

Pine Lake

At Milepost 722 (1 160 km), some 88 miles (140 km) from Watson Lake, a historic plaque describes the construction of the Pine Lake Airstrip, which augmented the air bases on the Alaska Highway in the Second World War. At that time, it was designated Flight Strip No. 5

This is a seasonal 3,250' (990 m) gravel airstrip still in use today, but serves more as an emergency strip or fishing stopover than anything else. It has limited maintenance and no services. The Rancheria River runs by it and there are a couple of lakes within walking distance to the north. Early prospectors from California gave this river its name (in Spanish it means farm).

Squanga Lake Airstrip, June 2000.

Teslin

This outpost on the Alaska Highway boasts an historic first. In 1928 George Johnston, an enterprising photographer, trapper, and Tlingit, acquired Teslin Lake's first automobile, a current-model Chevrolet. He then proceeded to build 3 miles (5 km) of road along the lake and charged for rides on his private "highway".

Today Teslin's airstrip has a 5500' (1 675 m) seasonal gravel strip.

Squanga Lake

This 6,100' (1 860 m) emergency airstrip was another part of the Northwest Staging Route. According to a Yukon Historic Sites' Survey conducted in the early 1990s, a family of eagles has taken over the field's old beacon. The lake is named after a species of whitefish—in Tagish native language, squanga means "small whitefish". During the Second World War, it was designated Flight Strip No. 6.

Champagne

No signs of the Second World War strip here. A hub construction camp halfway between Whitehorse and Haines Junction; there were a few permanent buildings here.

Teslin Airstrip, June 2000.

Haines Junction

This important intersection on the Alaska Highway also included a road to the coast and the Dalton Trail to gold fields to the north. Jack Dalton incorporated several Indian trails into a toll trail during the gold rush and patrolled his trail with rifle and threats to anyone who didn't want to ante up.

The airstrip at Haines Junction is surrounded by high mountains and is a seasonal 5000' (1 675 m) gravel airstrip. It is not a place for tourist pilots to fly into at night because of its proximity to high terrain.

Painting of old town of Aishihik, Yukon— previously next to the site of a World War II emergency strip.
—Courtesy Wm. Sinclair, Bruce McAllister Collection

A color infrared aerial photo of Haines Junction airstrip.

Aerial of Aishihik in October, 1943.
—Yukon Archives, Finnie Collection, 446

A RCAF Beech 18 Expediter at Aishihik before or early in World War II.
—Yukon Archives, F. Hamilton Collection, 81/151-6

Aishihik

A key stop on the Northwest Staging Route during the Second World War, this abandoned airstrip is on the north shore of the lake, about 62 miles (100 km) north of Haines Junction. During the war, this remote airstrip had a few barracks, unimaginative air force cooks and a band of wild horses. According to a local source, its runway is inhabited by gophers and is dangerous to land on.

Silver City

On the south shore of Kluane Lake, this airstrip takes its name after the nearby ghost town which still has some buildings remaining from the Kluane Gold Rush of 1903. In 1942 Silver City came back to life when the US Army used it as a construction camp. The airstrip today serves people who live in the area—especially for medical evacuations. The first claim at Silver City was credited to a character named Dawson Charlie, one of the first men to hit Klondike pay dirt. In the early 1900s a crude road was built between Silver City and Whitehorse.

Aerial photo of Silver City airstrip.

Burwash (Kluane Lake)

On Kluane Lake, this 6000' (1 830 m) gravel strip is near a Second World War crash site. The name Kluane means "big fish lake" in the native language and was an important fishing area even before the Europeans came into the area in the 1800s. In the early 1900s it was a supply hub for gold miners who worked nearby claims at Burwash Creek. Burwash is named after Major L.T. Burwash who recorded claims at nearby Silver City.

The lake is a prominent landmark for pilots en route to Alaska.

Snag

Seventeen miles (27 km) east of Northway as the crow flies, this was another airstrip for the Northwest Staging Route in the Second World War. Today the 6,000-foot (1 830-m) airstrip is for summer/emergency use only. Snag City, as the Indians named it, has the distinction of holding the lowest recorded temperature in North America. In January 1947, the temperature plunged to 81 degrees (F) below zero! Airliners passing overhead at that time sounded as though they were next door, as did the howling dogs in nearby native villages. Only 2,000' (610 m) of runway is currently being used because of some young willow growth.

Building Snag Airstrip in October, 1943.
—Yukon Archives/ Finnie Collection/447

Aerial of Burwash airstrip in 1949.

Aerial of Beaver Creek settlement in 1975. Its remoteness means less room and board choices for pilots– but better fishing!

Beaver Creek

The last link in the record eight-month construction of the Alaska Highway was Beaver Creek. After October 28, 1942, one could drive the entire highway. It has a customs post and a 3740' (1 140m) seasonal gravel airstrip one mile northwest of town. Beaver Creek has always been a good rival to Snag for record temperatures! When Snag set a North American record low of eighty-one below zero (F), it was seventy-five below (F) at Beaver Creek!

This remote town does much business helping motorists with flat tires and mechanical problems. In the old days motorists reported the depth of pot holes by how much of their vehicle was still above ground!

Tanacross

The Second World War control tower/ hangar building at this airstrip has reincarnated itself as an ice hockey rink in Fairbanks. There is not much evidence of its role as an alternate field during the war, but it has discovered a new lease on life as a Bureau of Land Management fire fighting base. This native settlement on the Tanana

River originally was a telegraph station. Its name originated from the telegraph lines crossing the river. Its existing airstrip became quite useful to the Air Force during the Second World War as an alternate and the two runways were lengthened to accommodate military aircraft.

Since that war ended, Northway has become much more important as an airfield to general aviation. But Northway's isolation and lack of access in 1941 made Tanacross a viable alternative field. It was easier and quicker to build. Before the Alaska Highway was built all construction materials had to be flown into Northway.

World War II control tower at Tanacross, Alaska. Today it has found a new life as an ice rink in Fairbanks, and the airstrip at Tanacross is used as a fire fighting base by the US government.
–Kansas State Historical Society, Topeka, KS

ENDNOTES

1 Doris Peterson, interviewed by Peter Corley-Smith and R. D. Turner in Atlin, 1995.

2 Florida A & M University (in "History of the Alcan Highway" website).

3 Wesley F. Craven and James L. Gate, Editors, *The Army Air Forces in World War II*, 1983, p. 154 and 155.

4 Brian Garfield, *The Thousand-Mile War: World War II in Alaska and the Aleutians*, 1969, p. 152.

5 Rudy Billberg (as told to Jim Rearden), *In the Shadow of Eagles*, p. 121.

6 Richard Ecke, "To Russia With Love," *Great Falls Tribune*, August 24, 1992.

7 Heath Twitchell, Lieut. Col. US Army, *The Decision to Build the Alaska Highway: How and Why it Was Made*. Report prepared for the Naval War College, Newport, R.I., 1977, p. 40.

8 Blake W. Smith, *Warplanes in Alaska & the Yukon*, 1998, p.249.

9 K. M. Molson, *Pioneering in Canadian Air Transport*, 1974, pp. 175-76. (In 1973, McLean was inducted into Canada's Aviation Hall of Fame for his contribution to the development of airports in Canada.)

10 Ken Coates, *North to Alaska*, 1992, p. 36.

11 Ira Harkey, *Pioneer Bush Pilot: The Story of Noel Wien*, 1974. p. 266.

12 *Ibid*, p. 265.

13 L. E. Janson, *Mudhole Smith: Alaska Flyer*, p. 84.

14 Stephen Mills and James Phillips, *Sourdough Sky*, 1960, p. 141.

15 Harkey, pp. 267-276.

16 Sam Side, interviewed by Bruce McAllister.

17 Bob Trail, interviewed by Bruce McAllister.

18 Shirlee Smith Matheson, *Flying the Frontiers*, 1994, p. 54.

19 J.F. Anderson, *Outlaw Pilot: True Adventures of "Midnight" Jimmy Anderson*, Vol. I, 1993, p. 3.

20 The second book is *Outlaw Pilot: More Adventures of Jimmy "Midnight" Anderson*, 1995.

21 Al Schneider, interviewed by Bruce McAllister.

22 Paula Lounsbury. "The Way West: Flying/Driving to Alaska," *COPA Flight Focus*, August 2000.

23 Instrument Flight Rules.

24 Celia M. Hunter, of Fairbanks, Alaska. Phone interview and correspondence with Peter Corley-Smith.

25 Paul Bachinger, "Flying the Alaska Highway in Mid-Winter," *Alaska Magazine*, January, 1972, pp. 16-18 & 24.

26 Heath Twitchell, *Northwest Epic: The Building of the Alaska Highway*, p. 21.

27 Gerri Young, *The Fort Nelson Story*, Fort Nelson Website.

28 Heath Twitchell, *Northwest Epic*, p. 43.

29 Heath Twitchell, *Northwest Epic*, p. 111.

30 John and Josie Piety, interviewed by Peter Corley-Smith and Bob Turner.

31 June Lunny, *Spirit of the Yukon*, 1992.

32 W. D. MacBride, *All My Rivers Flowed West: Tales of the Flathead, Columbia and Yukon Rivers*, 1991.

33 Heath Twitchell, *Northwest Epic*, p. 235.

34 Lavell Wilson, "Northway and Tanacross: Airports for the War Effort," *Alaska Geographic*, Vol. 22, November 4, p. 72.

35 Lavell Wilson, "Northway and Tanacross: Airports for the War Effort," *Alaska Geographic*, Vol. 22, November 4, p. 76.

36 L. E. Janson, *Mudhole Smith: Alaska Flyer*. Smith earned the nickname when he landed on soft ground near a mine, nosed over and his propeller dug into the ground. There was no damage but when, with some help, he had pulled the aircraft clear of the hole, he had to spend several hours digging the mud out from between the cooling fins of the exposed radial engine with a screwdriver and ended up wearing a good deal of it—much to the entertainment of the off-duty bystanders from the mine who spread the word far and wide.

37 Jean Potter, *The Flying North*, 1972.

38 Herb Noble, "The Amazing Radial," *Aviator Magazine*, October 2000, p. 12.

39 Courtesy Howard F. Smiley, who wrote this accunt in 1990 and gave us permission to use it.

40 The second person in the front was not a pilot: it was air engineer Frank Coulter; and there were two policemen, both constables with the British Columbia Provincial Police (BCPP).

41 In January 1943, Howard Smiley was rotated back from the Aleutians to the 3rd Air Force Training Command in the US and stationed at Avon Park, Florida. He ended his tour of active duty as Base Executive Officer, Lake Charles, La. Air Base in July 1945, and returned to the practice of law that he had left to join the Air Corps in 1940. In 1964, he resigned from the USAF Reserve as a Lieutenant-Colonel.

42 In the small, one-man detachments, the policeman doubled as a game warden.

43 Curiously, the authorities seemed as eager to retrieve the Norden bombsights as they were to rescue the crews. But perhaps in the context of the times, not so curious because the Americans, just after they came into the war, were almost paranoid about the security of this supposedly uncannily accurate device—they claimed the ability to put a bomb in a pickle barrel from 20,000 feet (6 000 m).

BIBLIOGRAPHY

BOOKS

Anderson, J.F. *Outlaw Pilot: True Adventures of Jimmy "Midnight" Anderson*. Writer's Den, Parksville, BC, 1993.

_____. *Outlaw Pilot II, More Adventures of Jimmy "Midnight" Anderson*. Writer's Den, Parksville, BC, 1995.

Billberg, Rudy (as told to Jim Rearden). *In The Shadow of Eagles: From Barnstormer to Alaska Bush Pilot, A Flyer's Story*. Alaska Northwest Books, Seattle, WA, 1992.

Bruder, Gerry. *Heroes of the Horizon: Flying Adventures of Alaska's Legendary Bush Pilots*. Alaska Northwest Books, Seattle, WA, 1991.

Coates, Ken S. & Morrison, W.R. *The Alaska Highway in World War II: The US Army of Occupation in Canada's Northwest*. University of Toronto, ON, 1992.

Coates, Ken S. *North to Alaska*. McClelland & Stewart, Toronto, ON, 1992.

Cole, Dennott. *Frank Barr: Bush Pilot in Alaska & The Yukon*. Alaska Northwest, Books, 1986, 1999 (Caribou Classics).

Cohen, Stan. *Alcan & Canol: A Pictorial History of The Two Great World War II Construction Projects*. Pictorial Histories, Missoula, MT, 1992.

_____. *The Forgotten War*, Missoula, MT, 1981 (4 Volumes).

Craven, Wesley & Cate, James L., Eds. *The Army Air Forces in World War II*. Vol. Seven, Edited by Office of Air Force History, Washington, DC, 1983.

Corley-Smith, Peter. *Bush Flying To Blind Flying: 1930-1940*. Sono Nis Press, Victoria, BC, 1993.

_____. *Pilots to Presidents*: British Columbia's Aviation Leaders: 1930-1960. Sono Nis Press, Victoria, BC, 2001.

Dale, John. *Snowshoes & Stethoscopes, Tales of Medicine & Flying in the Canadian North*. Daedalus Publishing, Nelson, BC, 1997.

Day, Beth. *Glacier Pilot: The Story of Bob Reeve and the Flyers Who Pushed Back Alaska's Air Frontiers*, Ballantine Books, NY, 1973 (originally published in 1957 by Holt, Rinehart & Winston).

Garfield, Brian. *The Thousand-Mile War: World War II in Alaska and The Aleutians*. Doubleday & Co., Garden City, NY, 1969.

Gott, Kay. *Women in Pursuit: A Collection & Recollection of Women Pursuit Pilots of the ATS*.

Harkey, Ira. *Pioneer Bush Pilot, The Story of Noel Wien*. University of Washington Press, Seattle, WA, 1974.

Hayes, Otis. *The Alaska-Siberia Connection: The World War II Air Route*. Texas A & M, 1996.

Helmericks, Harmon. *The Last of The Bush Pilots*. Alfred A. Knopf, New York, NY, 1977.

Hirschmann, Fred. *Bush Pilots of Alaska*. Graphic Arts Center Publishing, Portland, OR, 1989.

Janson, L. E. *Mudhole Smith: Alaska Flyer*. Northwest Publishing Co., Anchorage, AK, 1981.

Johnson, Kent & John Mullock. *Aviation Weather Hazards of BC & The Yukon*. Federal Minister of Environment, Canada, 1996.

Keddell, Georgina M. *Peace Lovin' Folks: Stories of Alaska Highway Pioneers*. Margie Graham Publishing, Merritt, BC, 1992.

Keith, Ronald A. *Bush Pilot With A Briefcase: The Happy-Go-Lucky Story of Grant McConachie*. Douglas & McIntyre, Vancouver, BC, 1972.

Larson, Norman Leonard. *Radio Waves Across Canada & Up The Alaska Highway*. Occasional Paper No. 25, Lethbridge Historical Society, Lethbridge, AB, 1992.

Long, Everett A. *Cobras Over The Tundra*. Ark Low Enterprises, October, 1992.

Lunny, June. *Spirit of the Yukon*, Caitlin Press, Prince George, BC, 1992.

MacBride, W.D. *All My Rivers Flowed West: Tales of The Flathead, Columbia and Yukon Rivers*. Beringian Books, Whitehorse, Yukon, 1991.

Matheson, Shirlee Smith. *Flying The Frontiers: A Half-Million Hours of Aviation Adventure*. Vol. I & II: Vol. I, Fifth House, Calgary, AB, 1994; Vol. II, Detselig Enterprises, Calgary, 1996.

Morrison, Lee B. *Out of The Wilderness: Restoring a Relic*. Military Aviation Preservation Society, MAPS Air Museum, North Canton, OH, 1995.

Mills, Stephen E. *Arctic War Planes: Alaska Aviation of World War II*. Bonanza Books, New York, NY, 1978.

_____, & James W. Phillips. *Sourdough Sky, A Pictorial History of Flights & Flyers in The Bush Country*. Bonanza Books, New York, NY, 1960.

Molson, Ken M. *Pioneering in Canadian Air Transport*, James Richardson & Sons Ltd., Winnipeg, MB, 1974.

Palmer, Henry R. *This Was Air Travel*. Superior Publishing Company, Seattle, WA, 1960.

Potter, Jean. *The Flying North*. Ballantine Books, A Comstock Edition, New York, NY, 1972.

Potts, F.E. *Potts' Guide to Bush Flying: Concepts and Techniques for the Pro*. 1st Edition, ACS Publishing, Tucson, AZ, 1993.

Remley, David A. *Crooked Road: The Story of the Alaska Highway*. McGraw-Hill, NY 1976.

Rossiter, Sean. *The Immortal Beaver: The World's Greatest Bush Plane*. Douglas & McIntyre, Vancouver, BC, 1996.

_____. *Otter & Twin Otter: The Universal Airplanes*. Douglas & McIntyre, Vancouver, BC, 1998.

Rychetnik, Joe. *Alaska's Sky Follies: The Funny Side of Flying in The Far North*. Epicenter Press, Seattle/Fairbanks, 1995.

Satterfield, Archie. *The Alaska Airlines Story*. Northwest Publishing Co., Anchorage, AK, 1981.

Schmidt, John, *This was no %v*nii Picnic: 2.3 Years of Wild & Woolly Mayhem in Dawson Creek*, Gorman & Gorman, Hanna, AB, 1991.

Smith, Blake. *War Planes to Alaska,* Hancock House, Surrey, BC, 1997

Snow, Crocker. Ed Pam Gleason. *Logbook: A Pilot's Life*. A Roger Warner Book, Brassey's, Washington & London, 1997.

Stone, Ted. *Alaska & Yukon History Along The Highway*. Red Deer College Press, Red Deer, AB, 1997.

Taylor, Michael, Ed. *Jane's Encyclopedia of Aviation*. Portland House, New York, NY, 1989.

Twitchell, Heath. *Northwest Epic: The Building of the Alaska Highway*. St. Martin's Press, New York, NY, 1992.

_____. *The Decision to Build the Alaska Highway: How and Why it Was Made*. Naval War College, Newport, RI, 1977.

Whitesitt, Larry L. *Flight of the Red Beaver: A Yukon Adventure*. Lawton Publishing Company, Spokane, WA, 1990.

Wonders, William C. *Alaska Highway Explorers: Place Names Along the Adventure Road*. Horsdal and Schubart, Victoria, BC, 1994.

Worthylake, Mary M. *Up In The Air*. Maverick Publications, 1979.

Whyard, Florence. *Ernie Boffa: Canadian Bush Pilot*. First Published by Alaska Northwest Publishing Co., 1984.

ARTICLES

Alaska Geographic, Vol. 22, No. 4. Special Issue. "World War II in Alaska," 1994.

"Alcan Trail Blazers," 648th Memorial Fund, Pittsburgh, PA, 1992.

Bachinger, Paul, "Flying the Alaska Highway in Mid-Winter," *Alaska Magazine*, January, 1972, pp. 16-18 & 24.

Ecke, Richard, "To Russia With Love," *Great Falls Tribune*, August 24, 1992.

"History of the Alcan Highway," Website, Black Archives Research Center Museum, Florida A & M University.

Lounsbury, Paula, "The Way West: Flying/Driving to Alaska," *COPA Flight Focus*, August 2000.

Noble, Herb "The Amazing Radial," *Aviator Magazine*, October 2000, p. 12.

Wilson, Lavell, "Northway and Tanacross: Airports for the War Effort," *Alaska Geographic*, Vol. 22, November 4, 1998, p. 72.

A longtime resident of the Colorado Rockies, **Bruce McAllister** is a semi retired freelance magazine photographer who has flown the Alaska Highway numerous times and has over 4600 hours of flight time (with commercial, multi-engine and instrument ratings). His assignments have taken him to such diverse places as the Amazon, Ghana, Kuwait, Iran, and Borneo. He has flown above the Arctic Circle several times and was the first photographer to do extensive photo coverage of the 1969 oil strike on Alaska's North Slope.

Bruce has also had a close encounter with a grizzly bear inside Denali National Park, hiked the Trail of '98 from Skagway to Lake Bennett, and survived the rigors of the Sourdough Rendezvous in Whitehorse, Yukon in 1971.

Born in India, educated in England, with degrees as a mature student from the University of Victoria and the University of Montana, **Peter Corley-Smith** served as an SOE pilot in the Royal Air Force in World War II, became in turn a miner, surveyor, cartographer, commercial helicopter pilot and college instructor before becoming a history curator. Since retirement, he has served as a Research Associate at the Royal British Columbia Museum. His previous books include *10,000 Hours: A Helicopter Pilot in the North*; *Helicopters: The B.C. Story* (with Dave Parker); *Barnstorming to Bush Flying; Helicopters in the High Country* (with Dave Parker); and *Bush Flying to Blind Flying*. His latest book is *Pilots to Presidents, British Columbia's Aviation Leaders, 1930-1960*.